Killer Joe

A Play

by Tracy Letts

A SAMUEL FRENCH ACTING EDITION

FOUNDED 1830

New York Hollywood London Toronto

SAMUELFRENCH.COM

ISBN   978-0-573-62736-1   Printed   in   U.S.A.   #13052

IMPORTANT BILLING AND CREDIT REQUIREMENTS

All producers of KILLER JOE *must* give credit to the Author of the Play in all programs distributed in connection with performances of the Play and in all instances in which the title of the Play appears for purposes of advertising, publicizing or otherwise exploiting the Play and/or a production. The name of the Author *must* also appear on a separate line, on which no other name appears, immediately following the title, and *must* appear in size of type not less than fifty percent the size of the title type.

The following must also appear in all programs distributed in connection with performances of the Play:

"Killer Joe" was produced Off-Broadway by
Darren Lee Cole and Scott Morfee in
Association with 29th Street Rep

The New York premiere of "Killer Joe" was staged by
29th Street Rep
(Tim Corcoran and David Mogentale, Artistic Directors) and
Darren Lee Cole on September 29, 1994

Killer Joe was originally produced by the Next Lab in Evanston, Illinois, on August 3, 1993. It was directed by Wilson Milam; the set and lighting designs were by Robert G. Smith; the costume design was by Laura Cunningham; the sound design was by Chris Peterson; the fight choreographer was Chuck Ccyle; and the stage manager was Justin Holmes. The cast was as follows:

Chris Smith	Michael Shannon
Sharla Smith	Holly Wantuch
Ansel Smith	Marc A. Nelson
Dottie Smith	Shawna Franks
Killer Joe Cooper	Paul Dillon

Killer Joe received its New York City premiere on September 29, 1994 at 29th St. Rep. It was produced by 29th St. Rep (Tim Corcoran and David Mogentale, Artistic Directors) and Darren Lee Cole. The production was directed by Wilson Milam; set design was by Richard Meyer; lighting design was by Jeremy Kumin; costume design was by Elizabeth Elkins; the production stage manager was Brad Rohrer. The cast was as follows:

Chris Smith	Thomas Wehrle
Sharla Smith	Linda June Larson
Ansel Smith	Leo Farley
Dottie Smith	Danna Lyons
Killer Joe Cooper	David Mogentale

Killer Joe was produced in New York by Darren Lee Cole and Scott Morfee on October 18, 1998. It was directed by Wilson Milam; the set design was by George Xenos; the lighting design was by Greg MacPherson; the costume design was by Jana Stauffer; the sound design was by Hired Gun/One Dream; the fight choreographer was J. David Brimmer; and the stage manager was Richard Hodge. The cast was as follows:

Chris Smith	Michael Shannon
Sharla Smith	Amanda Plummer
Ansel Smith	Marc A. Nelson
Dottie Smith	Sarah Paulson
Killer Joe Cooper	Scott Glenn

DEBTS

Acting: Fairuza Balk, Scott Glenn, Jan Leslie Harding, Sarah Paulson(!), Lori Petty, Amanda Plummer, Seth Ullian, Michelle Williams

Agenting: Danielle Ausrotas, Jason Fogelson

Artistic Directing: Ian Brown, Dexter Bullard, Dominic Dromgoole, Harriet Spizziri

Believing, with money: Gary and Teddi Cole, Kelly Curtis, Steve Martin

Casting: Kris Nicolau

Criticizing: Richard Christiansen

Designing: Tim Fletcher, Luke Grimm, One Dream, Chris Peterson, Bob Smith, Jana Stauffer, George Xenos

Potato Peeler Designing: Tim Reinhart

Familiarizing: M & P, S & S, D & D, G & G, G & G

Fighting: David Brimmer, Chuck Coyle

Producing: Michael Codron, Darren Lee Cole, Laura Cunningham, Scott Morfee

Publicizing: Shirley Herz

Stage Managing: Siofra Campbell, Richard Hodge, Justin Holmes, Adrian Pagan

Understudying: Christine Ashe, Allen Burroughs, Mim Drew, Mary Hammett

BIGGER DEBTS

Paul Dillon, Shawna Franks, Marc Nelson, Mike Shannon, Holly Wantuch, Eric Winzenried, and especially Wilson Milam: the six actors and director who helped create this play

Without their work, talent, faith and love, *Killer Joe* would not exist.

Killer Joe is dedicated to the memory and spirit of
Holly Wantuch, my partner, my conscious, my love.

How often have I lain beneath rain on a strange roof,
thinking of home?

Darl
from *As I Lay Dying*
by William Faulkner

PRODUCTION NOTES

No pre-show music. Only static from the t.v.

No "incidental" or "atmosphere" music within the scenes.

All music and sound should be sourced, with the exception of intermission, curtain call, and the scene changes (see below).

Blackouts between the scenes should be covered by the sound of the following scene. For example, Act Two, Scene One ends; blackout, sound of evangelist on house speakers; once scene change is completed, lights rise on Scene Two, and evangelist cross-fades from house speakers to on-stage radio.

Scene changes should be as quick and quiet as possible.

Lighting should appear to be sourced.

The final dinner is wholly improvised, and may take as long as two or three minutes.

As written, the final fight is a map of the dynamics of the scene. Directors and fight choreographers worth their salt will change it as necessary to meet their staging needs.

A NOTE TO THE PLAYERS

The published edition of KILLER JOE contains many stage directions designed to help a reader visualize this material. Although you will inevitably incorporate many of these stage directions into your production, you are encouraged to start from scratch, inhabit the characters, and make the play your own.

Ellipses (...) indicate an incomplete thought, or a trailing off.

Dashes (–) indicate an interruption and overlapping.

CHARACTERS

CHRIS SMITH:
    22 years old

SHARLA SMITH:
    Chris's stepmother, early thirties

ANSEL SMITH:
    Chris's father, 38 years old

DOTTIE SMITH:
    Chris's sister, 20 years old

KILLER JOE COOPER:
    Mid thirties

PLACE

A trailer home on the outskirts of Dallas, Texas.

Two entrances: a door leading outside, and a hallway leading to the bathroom and two bedrooms.

The living room occupies two-thirds of the set; the kitchen occupies one-third. There is no separation between the rooms, unless it is a small counter extending from the wall. The playing area should be quite small and cramped. A low ceiling is helpful.

The furnishings and decorations in the trailer are seedy and cheap; walls covered with ugly wood paneling; tattered, smoke-stained plastic shades covering the windows; kitchen filled with dirty, mismatched cups and utensils, many of them fast-food giveaways; a hide-a-bed, stained, torn, burned with cigarettes; a coffee table covered with fast-food debris, empty beer cans, and filled ashtrays; grimy refrigerator, filled almost solely with beer; a monstrous television, topped by a snarled and intricate antenna made of coat hangers and tin foil; Taco Bell refrigerator magnets, Dallas Cowboy cheerleader calendar, ZZ Top poster, and other detritus of the poor.

ACT I

Scene One

(Lights slowly rise: faint glow of the street lights bleeds through the window shades ... flickering ghost light spills from the t.v., tuned to snow.)
(Lightning. Thunder.)
(T-BONE, a neighbor's pit bull with a bad attitude and a chain a few links too long, snorts and barks ferociously outside.)
(Footsteps. Doorknob. Tap on the door.)

CHRIS. Dottie? *(Beat)* Dottie? *(The tap grows louder. T-BONE keeps barking.)* Dottie, wake up. It's me. *(The tap grows even louder. CHRIS raises his voice slightly, but he tries to be quiet.)* Come on, Dottie, it's me, goddamn it. Let me in. I'm cold. I gotta piss. Let me in. *(Pause. The voice impatient, almost yelling. The knock gets louder.)* Shut up, T-Bone! Dottie, goddamn it, wake up! Don't make me wake up the whole goddamn neighborhood! I'm about to piss in my pants! *(Pause. The voice bellows and the pounding on the door threatens to tear down the entire wall.)* GODDAMN IT, OPEN THIS GODDAMN DOOR BEFORE I BURN THIS WHOLE GODDAMN TRAILER PARK TO THE GROUND! GET OUTTA THAT FUCKIN' BED, RIGHT! FUCKIN'! NOW!

(During the above, SHARLA appears from the hallway and scampers to the door. She wears only a man's sweat-stained tee-shirt that falls above her ass.)

SHARLA. Hold on, hold on –

(She unlocks the door and CHRIS bursts in.)

9

CHRIS. Goddamn it – ! *(Sees SHARLA, heads down the hallway.)* Put some clothes on, for Christ's sake.

SHARLA. Well, hell, I didn't know who you were. *(But he's gone. We hear CHRIS's urine splash in the toilet bowl.)* Close the goddamn door!

(He doesn't. She gets a soda from the fridge, stocked only with a few Cokes, a dribble of milk, and a lot of beer. She finds a cigarette, lights it. CHRIS returns.)

CHRIS. Why don't you put somethin' on? My God –

SHARLA. I didn't know who you were –

CHRIS. You answer the door like that if you don't know –

SHARLA. Just relax, it's nothin' you haven't seen before, I'm sure –

CHRIS. Nothin' half of Dallas County hasn't seen before, Sharla –

SHARLA. – shut up –

CHRIS. – but that ain't the point. It's freezin' in here –

SHARLA. What do you want?

CHRIS. Is Dad here?

SHARLA. He's asleep.

CHRIS. Dottie's here, isn't she?

SHARLA. Everybody's asleep, it's almost 3:00 in the–

CHRIS. I can tell time, all right?

SHARLA. Adele throw you out?

CHRIS. Yes, goddamn it. I need to talk to Dad –

SHARLA. Why'd she throw you out? Did you – ?

CHRIS. – that bitch –

SHARLA. – hit her again?

CHRIS. No, I didn't – look, will you please put some clothes on?

SHARLA. My God, I never heard so much –

CHRIS. I'm sorry, it's just a bit distractin' tryin' to talk to your stepmother with her bush starin' you right in the face –

(ANSEL, wearing just his underwear, turns on the lights as he enters from the hallway.)

SHARLA. All right! Jesus –
CHRIS. Thank you.

(SHARLA whacks ANSEL as she exits. CHRIS has grabbed a beer from the fridge and pulled the pot stash from under the couch. He rolls a joint.)

ANSEL. Help yourself.
CHRIS. What'd you do, chop up some clover? Where'd you get this shit?
ANSEL. I bought it from you.
CHRIS. This is that?
ANSEL. What are you doin' here?
SHARLA. *(O.S.)* Adele threw him out!
ANSEL. So?! The boy can talk!
CHRIS. So I needed a place to stay, all right?
ANSEL. How come she threw you out?
CHRIS. It's a long story.
ANSEL. Sharla, get me a beer! *(During the following, ANSEL crosses to the t.v., flips channels, finds a monster truck rally.)* You didn't hit her again, did you – ?
CHRIS. No, goddamn it, I didn't hit her –

(SHARLA returns, wearing a pair of Ansel's underwear.)

SHARLA. It's not like you never hit her before –
CHRIS. I didn't hit her, okay?
SHARLA. So why'd she throw you out?
CHRIS. None of your goddamn business, Sharla –

SHARLA.	ANSEL.
Hey, I live here – !	Calm down –

CHRIS. Well, Jesus Christ, Dad, I get thrown out in the middle of the night, and I come over here and have to listen to your naked wife givin' me the third degree –
SHARLA. I'm not naked –

CHRIS. Why do you let her walk around here like that?

SHARLA.	ANSEL.
Like what?	It's the middle of the –

CHRIS. She answered the door with her beaver puckered out like it was tryin' to shake my hand –
SHARLA. Hush your mouth –
ANSEL. She didn't know who you were –
CHRIS. That's not the point, goddamn it! I don't want Dottie havin' to look at her own stepmother's pussy!
SHARLA. That's it! I'm goin' to bed! I've heard all – !
CHRIS. Good night.
SHARLA. *(Going for CHRIS.)* You listen to me – !
CHRIS. Good night. Sweet dreams.

SHARLA.	ANSEL.
Ansel – !	Hey now –

CHRIS. Don't let the bedbugs bite.
ANSEL. *(Between CHRIS and SHARLA.)* Stop it, Chris – !
SHARLA. He can stay here tonight – !

ANSEL.	CHRIS.
Sharla, honey, now don't get like that – !	Hey, I'll stay as long as I by God feel like!

SHARLA. – but if he stays any longer, I'm liable to hurt the little bastard!
ANSEL. Sharla, don't go to bed all mad –
SHARLA. Good night!

(She exits.)

CHRIS. *(Calling to her.)* Don't die in your sleep!
SHARLA. *(O.S.)* GODDAMN HICK!

(CHRIS lights the joint, takes a long drag, passes it to ANSEL. They smoke the joint throughout the scene.)

ANSEL. Now look what you did. I'm in the doghouse.

CHRIS. Fuck her.

ANSEL. Yeah, well, you don't live here –

CHRIS. I need to talk to you about somethin'.

ANSEL. I don't have any money for you –

CHRIS. I don't need a lot, but I'm in some trouble –

ANSEL. You're not listenin' to me, Chris –

CHRIS. – and if I can just get a little something to get me back on my feet –

ANSEL. No, goddamn it, you're not suckin' any more money outta me –

CHRIS. It's important, Dad –

ANSEL. It always is.

CHRIS. It's a matter of life and death, really.

ANSEL. It always is.

CHRIS. I need six thousand dollars, or some guys are gonna kill me.

ANSEL. Boy, you better get outta town, and quick.

CHRIS. If you could just give me a thousand –

ANSEL. – I don't have it –

CHRIS. I could hold these guys off with a thousand –

ANSEL. Chris. I don't have it.

CHRIS. I wouldn't be in this mess if it weren't for Mom, y'know –

ANSEL. Oh, I doubt that.

CHRIS. I'm in a jam cause of her, then she kicks me out.

ANSEL. Well, what'd you do to her? She wouldn'ta kicked you out for no reason –

CHRIS. She's a fuckin' bitch, Dad –

ANSEL. You hit her, didn't you?

CHRIS. Goddamn it, NO! I didn't hit her, I told you –

ANSEL. Then why'd she throw you out?

CHRIS. I threw her up against the fridge.

ANSEL. That's pretty much the same as hittin' her, wouldn't you say?

CHRIS. No, it's not. I barely threw her. There's not a mark on her.

ANSEL. But she threw you out anyway – ?

CHRIS. You wanna know why I threw her?

ANSEL. No.

CHRIS. She stole two and a half ounces of coke from me.

ANSEL. Now, that's bullshit. Your mother doesn't snort cocaine.

CHRIS. I know that, goddamn it, she sold it. Or gave it away to that goddamn Rex. Cause the shit was gone, and she's the only other one who knew where it was. Then tonight, after I find it missin', she comes back to the house with her Pinto runnin' like a watch.

ANSEL. You're shittin' me. That piece of shit hasn't run in years –

CHRIS. Y'see? What'd I tell you? So the blow I was plannin' on sellin' to pay these guys back is gone, and now they're gonna kill me. My own mother, for Chrissake. *(Beat)* So?

ANSEL. Hm? What?

CHRIS. The money. Are you gonna loan me the money?

ANSEL. No.

CHRIS. That's great. That's just great. You're a regular what's-his-name. I'm fucked –

ANSEL. I never had a thousand dollars in my life –

CHRIS. How would you like to?

ANSEL. What?

CHRIS. Would you like to have fifteen thousand dollars?

ANSEL. Aw, Jesus, another one of your stupid –

CHRIS. Now just hear me out, I got another plan here –

ANSEL. Every goddamn time. How about that farm – ?

CHRIS. Hey, now just leave the farm out of it, all right? I'm talkin' about somethin' a lot easier than that.

ANSEL. This oughta be good –

CHRIS. You ever hear of Killer Joe Cooper?

ANSEL. Huh-uh.

CHRIS. He's a cop.

ANSEL. Yeah?

CHRIS. Well, a detective, actually.

ANSEL. Yeah?

CHRIS. And he's got a little business on the side.
ANSEL. What's he do?
CHRIS. He's a killer. He kills people.
ANSEL. Yeah? So?
CHRIS. Mom's got a fifty-thousand dollar life insurance policy.

(Beat)

ANSEL. What are you sayin'?
CHRIS. You know what I'm sayin'. Don't look at me like that.
ANSEL. Who's the ... ?
CHRIS. Beneficiary. Dottie.
ANSEL. The whole thing?
CHRIS. The whole thing.
ANSEL. All fifty-thousand?
CHRIS. Yep.
ANSEL. She didn't leave nothin' to me?
CHRIS. Of course not, you dipshit. Why would she do that?
ANSEL. I'm her ex-husband.
CHRIS. She hates you, Dad. You know that.
ANSEL. Yeah, but still –
CHRIS. What do you think?
ANSEL. About what?
CHRIS. My idea.
ANSEL. How much does a thing like that cost?
CHRIS. I hear he charges twenty-thousand.
ANSEL. Jesus Christ –
CHRIS. This really isn't somethin' we can afford to cut corners on. I'd say it's worth it if we know we're not gonna get caught. Killer Joe's a professional, and he'll do this right.
ANSEL. How do you know? Who told you about this?
CHRIS. Never mind that.
ANSEL. Where are we supposed to get that kind of money?
CHRIS. I wanna hire him on spec. Ask him to do it for free, then give him a cut of the insurance money.
ANSEL. Look, after you pay this guy, you're only talkin' about clearin' ...

ANSEL.   CHRIS.
... thirty thousand.   ... thirty thousand.
Split that four ways –

CHRIS. Three ways.
ANSEL. How do you figure?
CHRIS. You, me, and Dottie.
ANSEL. What about Sharla?
CHRIS. What about her?
ANSEL. She gets a cut.
CHRIS. The hell she does. She's not family.
ANSEL. She's been my wife longer than Adele has.
CHRIS. It's less money.
ANSEL. It's less money for you.
CHRIS. And it's more money for you.
ANSEL. Yeah? I am the father here, y'know. We're talkin' about my ex-wife. I'm the one who found her. Not you, and not Dottie.
CHRIS. Okay, all right, fine, we can split it four ways –
ANSEL. Hold on just a second here. I haven't agreed to nothin' yet. This is murder we're talkin' about, and I'm not just gonna sit here, noddin' my head –
CHRIS. Look at it this way. Is she doin' anybody any good?
ANSEL. Whattaya mean?
CHRIS. Is anybody gonna really care if Mom's not around anymore?
ANSEL. Rex.
CHRIS. You think that dumb son-of-a-bitch would care? He screws anything that can draw breath –
ANSEL. That don't mean he don't care –
CHRIS. Tell you the truth, I think he'd be tickled pink. You should see how she treats that poor bastard.
ANSEL. 'Bout like she treated me, I bet.
CHRIS. Anyway, who gives a fuck about Rex?
ANSEL. Right –
CHRIS. Who else?
ANSEL. Dottie, maybe.
CHRIS. Right, Dottie. Now think of it this way: which do you

think would be better for Dottie, havin' ten thousand dollars so maybe she could go to that Amazon school, or havin' a beat-up, old, ugly, naggy alcoholic mother for another twenty years or so?

ANSEL. I see what you're sayin' –

CHRIS. Exactly. So as long as Dottie never knows what we're talkin' about ... we're really doin' her a favor.

ANSEL. Yeah ...

CHRIS. Let me just call him. Let's just set up a meetin' with the guy, and talk to him. We don't have to decide anything right now.

ANSEL. Okay.

CHRIS. Okay. Okay. Okay, good. Okay, now this's just between you and me, now.

ANSEL. I know.

CHRIS. Cause if Sharla or Dottie find out –

ANSEL. – right –

CHRIS. – they'll be considered accomplices –

(DOTTIE enters, wearing a night gown and robe.)

DOTTIE. Hey, Chris. What're you doin' here?

CHRIS. I got in a fight with Mom.

DOTTIE. Did you build this city all by yourself?

CHRIS. What? Uh, yeah. Sure did. Brick by brick.

DOTTIE. I heard that at the wedding.

ANSEL. *(To CHRIS.)* She's asleep.

DOTTIE. I'm not asleep, I'm just workin'.

(She exits.)

CHRIS. You think she heard us? *(ANSEL shrugs.)* Scared the shit outta me. That sleep-talkin' gives me the creeps.

ANSEL. She's gotten worse and worse about it. 'Bout every night now.

CHRIS. I don't suppose she's seein' anybody yet.

ANSEL. No, and I wouldn't hold your breath, neither.

CHRIS. I don't understand it.

ANSEL. You wanna know the truth, I think she's still ... you know ...

CHRIS. What. A virgin?

(She reenters, gets a comic book.)

DOTTIE. I heard y'all talkin' about killin' Momma. *(Beat)* I think it's a good idea.

(She exits. Beat.)

CHRIS. There you go.
ANSEL. Yeah ...
CHRIS. ... so ...

(Long silence.)

ANSEL. She got that piece of shit Pinto runnin' again, huh?

(Blackout.)
(Sound of the karate movie from the next scene plays over the blackout.)

Scene Two

(Lights rise.)
(Two days later: the shades are up and daylight streams through the window. Rain falls outside ... an occasional distant rumble of thunder.)
(DOTTIE is alone, "exercising" in the living room, matching moves with an action sequence from a poorly dubbed karate movie on t.v. The volume is ear-splitting.)
(The door to the trailer opens and KILLER JOE COOPER enters, wearing a raincoat and cowboy hat. DOTTIE does not hear him. He shuts the door, stands motionless, watches her.)

JOE. Looks hard.

(She sucks in her breath, runs into the kitchen. They shout to be heard over the television.)

DOTTIE. Jesus – !

JOE. I didn't mean – !

DOTTIE. Who are you?!

JOE. Joe Cooper, I'm a friend of – ! Joe Cooper – ! Excuse me! *(Turns off t.v.)* Joe Cooper, I'm a friend of –

DOTTIE. How'd you get in here?

JOE. The door. I knocked, but you had the t.v. turned up too loud to hear me. I decided not to stand in the rain.

DOTTIE. Well, you scared me to death –

JOE. And I apologize.

DOTTIE. That's okay. It's okay.

JOE. Looks hard. From the t.v. like that. You should get a teacher.

DOTTIE. Yeah ...

JOE. *(Extends his hand.)* I'm Joe Cooper.

DOTTIE. *(Shakes his hand.)* Hi.

JOE. I was supposed to meet Chris here at 10:30.

DOTTIE. He's not here.

JOE. I'm a little early.

DOTTIE. He's usually late.

JOE. *(Beat)* Could I trouble you for a cup of coffee, or – ?

DOTTIE. Oh, yeah, sure. I'm sorry. Why'n'tcha sit down? Can I take your – ?

(JOE removes his raincoat and hands it to DOTTIE, who drapes it over the back of a chair. She prepares a pot of coffee.)

JOE. Can I ask your name?

DOTTIE. I'm Dottie.

JOE. Hello, Dottie.

DOTTIE. Hi. *(He stands, stares at her. She feels his eyes on her, wheels, faces him.)* What.

JOE. Hm?

DOTTIE. Why are you – what?

JOE. Nothin'. I'm just ... standin'.

DOTTIE. Okay. *(Beat)* What are you? I mean, what do you do?

JOE. I'm a detective.

DOTTIE. Really? Like Mannix?

JOE. Uh ... no. He's a private detective. I'm in the Dallas Police Department.

DOTTIE. He's not real, either.

JOE. No. I'm real.

DOTTIE. I read it's nothin' like the shows, with car chases and all.

JOE. Lot of paperwork.

DOTTIE. I read some policemen go their whole lives without shooting their guns.

JOE. Probably true.

DOTTIE. Have you ever drawn your gun?

JOE. Oh, sure.

DOTTIE. What happened?

JOE. I've drawn my gun lots of times.

DOTTIE. You ever shot anybody?

JOE. Yes.

DOTTIE. Who?

JOE. Nobody you'd know.

DOTTIE. Did they die?

JOE. They have, yes.

DOTTIE. Wow. I bet you don't like to talk about it.

JOE. No, no. Not that I like to talk about it, but it doesn't keep me up nights. You know.

DOTTIE. Yeah. *(Beat)* What's the most exciting thing that ever happened?

JOE. Hm. The most exciting. I don't know. I don't know.

DOTTIE. *(Beat)* I bet it's more exciting than anything I ever –

JOE. Oh, wait, I can tell you the funniest thing –

DOTTIE. – okay –

JOE. – well, maybe not the funniest, but the ... oddest.

DOTTIE. Okay –

JOE. When I was a patrolman – do you want to hear this?

DOTTIE. Yeah, sure –

JOE. When I was a patrolman, my partner and I got a call there was a domestic disturbance in progress. Which is kind of misleading, if you ask me, because "domestic" sounds awful homey, and "disturbance" sounds like just an argument. But cops know that domestic disturbances are the calls where you're most likely to get hurt.

DOTTIE. Uh-huh.

JOE. So we took the call, and I was a little nervous. (I hadn't been on the force long, and I still got nervous about domestic disturbances.) When we got to the house, we heard this awful screaming from inside, this shrieking.

DOTTIE. Wow.

JOE. We went into the place, and it was completely dark, and we just followed the sound of this scream back to the back bedroom. I didn't know what the hell to expect –

DOTTIE. – yeah –

JOE. – and we open the door, and suddenly, this huge guy is on top of me, knocks me to the floor, just screaming and clawing at me –

DOTTIE. Oh my God –

JOE. And then it turns out ... there's no one else even there. And he wasn't trying to hurt me ... he wanted me to help him.

DOTTIE. Why?

JOE. He was in terrible pain. It turns out ... he had gotten into a fight with his girlfriend. She had been having an affair ... so, in order to "teach her a lesson," (that's what he said, "teach her a lesson") he had doused his genitals with lighter fluid, and set them on fire.

(DOTTIE stares at JOE. He laughs. She joins in the laughter.)

DOTTIE. Oh, I get it. I thought you were serious.

JOE. I am. *(She stops laughing. He continues.)* That poor, miserable bastard set his genitals on fire to teach his girlfriend a lesson. Do you believe that? Guess he showed her. I wonder if she ever got over it.

DOTTIE. Was he all right?

JOE. No. No, he wasn't all right. He set his genitals on fire. *(Beat)* Oh, boy.

DOTTIE. I had an aunt who set herself on fire –

JOE. Yeah, okay –

DOTTIE. – but not on purpose. She was wearin' a long lace dress and she got it caught in the furnace and she died before they put out the fire.

JOE. Really.

(She pours his coffee.)

DOTTIE. They say she's the one in the family I look most like.

JOE. Hm.

DOTTIE. Her name was Viva. Isn't that a great name? She never got married, I don't think. *(She hands him his coffee.)* Are you gonna kill my momma?

JOE. I'm not sure. Why?

DOTTIE. Just curious. *(Beat)* My momma tried to kill me when I was real little. She put a pillow over my face and tried to stop me from breathing, 'cause she cared more about herself than her little baby, and she didn't love me like a mother loves a little baby. And she thought she'd done it, and she was happy, 'cause then she didn't have to worry about me eating her food, and sleeping in her bed, and growing up to be the part of her that was cut out and grown into a better thing than she had been, had ever been. 'Cause that would mean the best part of her was me. But she hadn't done it, she didn't give me back to Him, she only made me sick, made me not be for a while, but then I was and she was sad that I was, and that I always would be.

(T-BONE barks as CHRIS and ANSEL approach from outside.)

JOE.	CHRIS.
(Studies her for a moment, then:)	*(O.S., laughing.)*
How do you know that?	You charged him how much?

DOTTIE.	ANSEL.
Know what?	*(O.S.)*
	Fifty bucks.

JOE.
That your mother tried to
kill you.

CHRIS.
(O.S.)
For a lousy spark plug!

DOTTIE.
'Cause I remember.

ANSEL.
(O.S.)
Hell, he didn't know the
difference, dumbass
Yankee.

(CHRIS enters, soaking wet. ANSEL, dressed in grease-stained auto mechanic's overalls, is behind CHRIS on the stairs, so he does not see JOE standing in the kitchen.)

ANSEL. About sucked my dick for havin' the right-sized wrench.

(ANSEL now sees JOE and freezes behind CHRIS.)

JOE. Hello.
CHRIS. Oh, Jesus, you must be Joe. *(CHRIS goes to him and they shake hands.)* Chris Smith. This is my father, Ansel.
JOE. *(Shaking hands with ANSEL.)* Ansel.
ANSEL. Hey there.
CHRIS. I guess you met Dottie.
JOE. Oh, yes.
CHRIS. Dottie, would you excuse us?
DOTTIE. Yeah, sure.
CHRIS. I mean, could you leave the house? We've got some business to discuss with Mr. –
DOTTIE. I know. *(To JOE.)* Good-bye.
JOE. Good-bye, Dottie.

(She grabs her coat and JOE opens the door for her. She exits, giving JOE a final look.)

CHRIS. *(In the fridge, getting beers.)* She's a sweetheart, isn't she?

JOE. Yes, she is.

CHRIS. Like a beer?

JOE. No ... no, listen, I don't have a lot of time –

CHRIS. All right, sir, let's get down to it.

JOE. If that's all right –

CHRIS. First off, let me say that me and my father here have never done anything like this before, and ... well, to be honest, we don't want to do it, but it's gotta be done.

JOE. That has nothing to do with me.

CHRIS. Okay. Uhh .... well, sir, instead of me starting this off, maybe you could sort of tell us the questions we need to ask, or –

JOE. It's really pretty simple. You're going to pay me some money for a service I'm going to perform.

CHRIS. Uh-huh.

JOE. You'll give me particulars about her whereabouts, her schedule, her habits, and I'll act on them accordingly. I won't give you many details about my activities, because the less you know about them, the better for everyone concerned.

CHRIS. All right –

JOE. I only have a couple of rules that I insist on sticking to. Insist.

CHRIS. Okay, yeah –

JOE. If you are caught, if you are implicated in this crime, you are not, under any circumstances, to reveal my identity or my participation.

CHRIS. Oh, of course –

JOE. If you break this rule, you'll be killed. Do you understand?

CHRIS. I –

JOE. I don't mean to sound melodramatic, and I don't want our business relationship to get off on the wrong foot. But I want to be absolutely clear on this point.

CHRIS. I understand.

JOE. *(To ANSEL.)* Do you understand?

ANSEL. Yeah.

JOE. My payment is twenty-five thousand dollars, in cash, in advance. No exceptions.

ANSEL. Twenty-five?

JOE. Yes, sir.

ANSEL. *(To CHRIS.)* You told me twenty.

CHRIS. *(To ANSEL.)* I was told twenty.

JOE. Twenty-five. Is that a problem?

CHRIS. We don't have a problem with twenty-five –

ANSEL. Now hold on a second here –

CHRIS. We don't have a problem with twenty-five. That's not our problem.

JOE. What is your problem?

CHRIS. We have a problem with the advance.

JOE. No exceptions.

CHRIS. Sir. I'd just like ... let me explain. One of the reasons we're interested in having this done is that my mother holds a very large insurance policy –

JOE. *(Standing to leave.)* They usually do.

CHRIS. – and we thought we could interest you in the job if we guaranteed payment after the policy had been covered.

JOE. This really isn't open to discussion. Our conversation is finished.

(JOE gets his coat, moves for the door. CHRIS reaches for him ...)

CHRIS. Please, this is important –

(... JOE turns and fires:)

JOE. What did you think this was? "Let's Make a Deal"? This is serious business you're fuckin' with here, boy –

CHRIS. I'm aware of that –

JOE. I don't think you are. I don't take you seriously.

CHRIS. This is gonna get done, one way or another –

JOE. Our conversation ... is finished. I never met you. You never met me. *(CHRIS gives up, goes to the kitchen. To ANSEL.)* Thank Dottie for the coffee. *(JOE turns to the door, his back to the room. Long pause. He slowly turns around to face CHRIS and ANSEL.)* Of course, we never discussed the possibility of a retainer.

CHRIS. Whattaya mean?

JOE. You know how to reach me. Call me if she's interested.

(Again, he starts for the door.)

CHRIS. Hey, man, are you talkin' about my sister?
JOE. Is that who she is?

(JOE exits. During the following, ANSEL checks JOE from the window, lights a joint, turns on the t.v., finds some auto racing.)

CHRIS. Jesus –
ANSEL. What's he mean, "retainer?"
CHRIS. Whattaya think he means, Dad? He means Dottie.
ANSEL. Yeah, but retain what, exactly?
CHRIS. Just how stupid are you? Are you really that stupid?

(ANSEL grabs a plastic troll, hurls it at CHRIS's head. CHRIS dodges, and the troll smashes into the wall.)

ANSEL. You watch your goddamn mouth!
CHRIS. What are we gonna do, Dad? We gotta think of somethin'.
ANSEL. We could do it ourselves.
CHRIS. You gonna kill somebody? You can't even tell time.
ANSEL. What do you think we should do, smart ass?
CHRIS. We can forget about the whole thing, or we can ... give him Dottie.
ANSEL. GODDAMN IT! *(ANSEL jumps off the couch, fusses with the t.v. antenna until his reception improves. Then:)* Y'know, it might just do her some good.

(Blackout.)
(Sound of the lottery drawing from the next scene plays over the scene change.)

Scene Three

(Lights rise.)
(SHARLA talks on the telephone, smiling, examining a sheaf of photographs. She wears the red-and-white checkered uniform of a Pizza Hut waitress. The Texas Lottery drawing plays on t.v.)

SHARLA. Don't be silly. Nobody's gonna see 'em. *(Beat)* What're you so worried about, anyway? It's not like you can see your face in any of 'em. *(Laughs)* I doubt it. *(Beat)* That little photo shack out in front of the mall. *(Beat)* Oh, hell, you worry too much. Just some little pimply-faced girl, never saw one before in her life. *(Beat)* None that big, anyway. *(Nasty laugh.)* What time are you gonna pick me up? *(Beat)* 11:30? What do you expect me to – ? *(DOTTIE comes out of her bedroom, wearing a pair of blue jeans and a sweatshirt, crosses to the t.v., changes channels, finds "Wheel of Fortune." SHARLA casually puts the photographs in a rainbow-colored packet.)* Hold on, Jennie. *(SHARLA covers the phone and speaks to DOTTIE, who is now setting the table for supper.)* Why don't you put on your new dress, hon?
DOTTIE. What for?
SHARLA. We're havin' a guest for supper.
DOTTIE. Who?
SHARLA. I don't know. Some friend of Ansel's. *(Back to phone.)* Huh? No, it's Dottie –
DOTTIE. We have to dress up?
SHARLA. I just think you look real pretty in your dress.
DOTTIE. I'd rather save it for somethin' special. I'd feel silly just wearin' it for supper.

(SHARLA pauses, then returns to the phone.)

SHARLA. Jennie? I'll call you from work, all right? No, I can't – no, I have to – uh-huh, you me, too. *(SHARLA hangs up, sticks her finger into a hole in DOTTIE's sweatshirt.)* Look at that.
DOTTIE. What? It's a sweatshirt.
SHARLA. Why don't you put on your dress?

DOTTIE. I don't feel like it. Is everybody else dressin' up?

SHARLA. I don't know what everybody else's doin'. I'm goin' to work.

DOTTIE. Then what difference does it make?

SHARLA It doesn't, really. Your daddy just wanted you to look nice.

DOTTIE. Where are they?

SHARLA. They'll be here. They better be. I gotta get to work. *(SHARLA prepares for work, putting on make-up, fixing her hair.)* What're you fixin'?

DOTTIE. Just some casserole.

SHARLA. What kind? Smells like tuna.

DOTTIE. It is.

SHARLA. You gonna make a salad?

DOTTIE. I could, if people're hungry enough.

SHARLA. Some rolls or somethin'?

DOTTIE. No.

SHARLA. I think we got some biscuits in there.

DOTTIE. We got plenty.

SHARLA. Okay. I was just sayin' ...

DOTTIE. Was that your boyfriend on the phone?

SHARLA. What do you mean?

DOTTIE. Wasn't that your boyfriend?

SHARLA. I'm married, silly.

DOTTIE. I won't tell Daddy.

SHARLA. I don't know what you're talkin' about. That was Jennie, my friend from high school.

DOTTIE. Is he cute?

SHARLA. Stop talkin' like that.

DOTTIE. I hope he's cute. You should have a cute boyfriend.

SHARLA. Listen –

DOTTIE. I had a boyfriend in the third grade, but I never told nobody. His name was Marshall and he was fat. But he loved me.

SHARLA. You should go out more often –

DOTTIE. It was our little secret, me and Marshall. All the other kids would always make a big show of goin' together, writin' their initials on their notebooks and holdin' hands at recess, but me and

Marshall kept it a secret. Nobody at that school ever knew we were goin' together and nobody at home knew either, even though nobody ever asked. We never saw each other at recess and we didn't have any lunch together and we didn't write notes and he didn't walk me home from school.

SHARLA. When would you see him?

DOTTIE. In class. At school.

SHARLA. I mean alone.

DOTTIE. We didn't see each other alone.

SHARLA. Ever?

DOTTIE. That would've spoiled the secret.

SHARLA. How did you all decide you were goin' together if you never spent any time alone?

DOTTIE. We just knew.

SHARLA. Wait –

DOTTIE. We never had to talk about it. If we'd talked about it, it wouldn't've been what it was, which was true.

SHARLA. What was true?

DOTTIE. Love. We loved each other.

SHARLA. How do you know he loved you if y'all never talked about it?

DOTTIE. He loved me with a pure love.

SHARLA. Well, there's not many like that around, I guess.

DOTTIE. It's Joe, isn't it? Joe's comin' over.

SHARLA. Joe who?

DOTTIE. I don't remember. His eyes hurt.

SHARLA. Huh?

DOTTIE. What?

SHARLA. I don't remember his name, but it was important to Ansel you put on your dress. I guess he wanted to make a good impression. *(Beat)* You met him?

DOTTIE. Uh-huh.

SHARLA. What's he like?

DOTTIE. He told me I should get a teacher for my kung fu.

SHARLA. Yeah ...

DOTTIE. He had me make him some coffee.

SHARLA. What's he like?

DOTTIE. I don't know ...

SHARLA. *(Beat)* Well. Anyway. Why don't you put on your dress?

DOTTIE. Okay.

(T-BONE barks outside.)

SHARLA. And you just forgot about Jennie, all right? She's just an old friend and I don't wanna have any trouble with your daddy over an old friend.

DOTTIE. You should have a cute boyfriend.

(ANSEL enters.)

SHARLA. I bet your ears were burnin'.

ANSEL. You all talkin' about me?

DOTTIE. No, sir –

SHARLA. I was just tellin' Dottie how you wanted her to put on her dress for dinner tonight.

ANSEL. *(As he changes channels on t.v., finds an episode of "Cannon.")* Would you, honey?

DOTTIE. Is everybody dressin' up?

ANSEL. Yeah. Yeah, we're all gonna dress up.

DOTTIE. Okay.

(She exits.)

SHARLA. Ansel Ray, get in this kitchen.

ANSEL. What?

SHARLA. When are you gonna tell that girl?

ANSEL. Tell her what?

SHARLA. That it's just gonna be her and Joe.

ANSEL. She's not stupid. She'll figure it out.

SHARLA. You gotta tell her. She doesn't know what to expect.

ANSEL. There's nothin' to expect –

SHARLA. That girl's not like other people, goddamn it. She doesn't put two and two together, like you and me and Chris –

ANSEL. There's nothin' to get worried over –

SHARLA. She's never even been on a real date before –

ANSEL. It's not a date –

SHARLA. Well it's the closest thing she ever had to one, except for some fat kid who didn't even know it –

ANSEL. What fat kid?

SHARLA. Give me the keys. I gotta get to work.

ANSEL. There's no reason to get all bent outta –

SHARLA. You talk to that girl, Ansel, cause you're liable to blow this thing real good –

ANSEL. *(Fishing keys out of pocket.)* What'm I gonna say?

SHARLA. Tell her the story, for God's sake. Don't make everything so complicated –

ANSEL. What story?

SHARLA. The situation. Tell her why he's comin' over tonight.

(He is having difficulty extracting the keys from his pocket.)

ANSEL. How the hell am I supposed – ?

SHARLA. I don't know, but if she – look at it this way, if she doesn't know why he's – what've you got in your pockets?!

ANSEL. It's like gum or somethin' –

SHARLA. If she doesn't know what's expected of her, then she might disappoint him. Now did you think of that?

ANSEL. I can't tell the girl how to behave –

SHARLA. Oh, you can't tell anybody anything! Give me those goddamn keys!

(He finally jerks the keys from his pocket, along with a shower of loose change that falls to the kitchen floor. She snaps the keys from his hand, flings the door open –)

ANSEL. Wait, Sharla – (– and leaves. ANSEL steps out, calls after her.) – what fat kid?! (Then, to a neighboring trailer:) Would you tie up that fuckin' dog?! (Unseen to us, the dog attacks. ANSEL retreats quickly into the trailer, slams the door just in time. T-BONE snaps and growls outside, but eventually gives up. ANSEL angrily picks up a chair, considers throwing it, reconsiders, becomes hypnotized by the cop show on t.v.) Cannon, you fat bastard ...

(He stops, collects his change, pockets it, gets a beer from the fridge, kills a bug, cackles as he washes its remains down the sink. DOTTIE enters, wearing a sexy black evening dress.)

DOTTIE. Daddy?

ANSEL. Oh, honey ...

DOTTIE. What do you think?

ANSEL. You look like a goddamn movie star. Come on over here. *(He grabs a chair, helps her stand on it.)* Turn around. *(She does.)* Like a goddamn movie star.

DOTTIE. I feel funny.

ANSEL. Why?

DOTTIE. I don't know. I feel like I went to school naked, like that dream you told me about.

ANSEL. Don't feel funny. You're beautiful.

DOTTIE. My butt's too big.

ANSEL. Let me let you in on a little secret: guys like big butts.

DOTTIE. They do not.

ANSEL. *(Feeling her butt.)* I'm speakin' from experience.

DOTTIE. *(Getting down from chair.)* Sharla doesn't have a big butt.

ANSEL. Give her some time.

DOTTIE. Why aren't you dressed yet?

ANSEL. I'm not gonna stay for dinner.

DOTTIE. What do you mean?

ANSEL. Me and Chris have some business to attend to –

DOTTIE. Where's Chris?

ANSEL. He's on his way –

DOTTIE. Then where –

ANSEL. So it's just gonna be you and Joe for dinner.

DOTTIE. *(Beat)* I should change.

ANSEL. No –

DOTTIE. Yeah, I should –

ANSEL. No, I think it'd be nice for Joe if he –

DOTTIE. Yeah, I'm gonna go change –

(She heads back to the bedroom. ANSEL grabs her arm.)

ANSEL. Whoa, whoa, hold up, honey –
DOTTIE. Let me go, I need to change –
ANSEL. Just listen for a second –
DOTTIE. I have to change – *(She tries to pull away, but ANSEL grabs her around the waist. T-BONE barks again.)* I have to change, I have to change, I have to change –
ANSEL. Now, calm down, Dottie, just –
DOTTIE. I have to change, I have to change –
ANSEL. *(More violent.)* Hold still, you little bitch – !
DOTTIE. *(Hysterical)* I HAVE TO CHANGE!

(CHRIS bursts in, immediately separates ANSEL and DOTTIE. She collapses to the floor.)

CHRIS. What the hell's goin' on – ?!
ANSEL. She wants to get out of her dress!
CHRIS. So?!
ANSEL. Well, I told her I thought it'd be nice for Joe if – !
CHRIS. Let her change if she wants!
ANSEL. Don't you think she looks nice?!
CHRIS. *(To DOTTIE.)* You put on whatever you like –
ANSEL. Now wait a goddamn second – !
CHRIS. Let her change, Dad –
ANSEL. Who the hell do you think – ?!

(CHRIS is suddenly in ANSEL's face.)

CHRIS. LET HER CHANGE! *(To DOTTIE.)* Go change.

(She exits down the hall.)

ANSEL. She looked great.
CHRIS. It's bad enough we gotta give the son-of-a-bitch a present. We don't have to gift-wrap it.
ANSEL. You listen to me –
CHRIS. This whole thing makes me sick.
ANSEL. This is my home –

CHRIS. You don't have a home –
ANSEL. – and I call the shots around here –
CHRIS. Shut up.
ANSEL. Just so you know.
CHRIS. She knows it's just gonna be the two of 'em?
ANSEL. She does now.
CHRIS. Great. Goddamn it. Too bad he didn't meet Sharla first, huh? He coulda dated her instead, and I wouldn'ta minded –
ANSEL. That's my wife you're talkin' about.
CHRIS. Yeah, right.
ANSEL. Look, are you ready? Joe told us to be gone half an hour ago.
CHRIS. Fuck Joe.
ANSEL. He's runnin' this show, ain't he?
CHRIS. I'll leave when I by God feel like it.
ANSEL. Chris ... ? If we're gonna do this, we should do it right.
CHRIS. Yeah, okay. *(A knock at the door.)* Poop.
ANSEL. Dottie?
DOTTIE. *(O.S.)* I'm not ready!
CHRIS. Answer the door, for God's sake.

(ANSEL opens the door and KILLER JOE enters, wearing a double-breasted suit, a new cowboy hat, and a pair of lizard-skin boots. He carries a bouquet of spring flowers.)

JOE. What are you doing here?
CHRIS. We're on our way out.
JOE. We discussed this –
CHRIS. Don't push it, we're leavin' –
JOE. Hey. That's right, Junior. Don't push it. When we make arrangements, I expect the details to have some attention paid to them.
CHRIS. Let's go, Dad.
JOE. You understand me?
CHRIS. Yeah ...
JOE. Good boy. Where is she?
CHRIS. She's changing.

(CHRIS and ANSEL leave. T-BONE barks. JOE takes off his hat, holds it, calls into DOTTIE's bedroom.)

JOE. Dottie? It's me, Joe Cooper. We're alone now. *(Beat)* It's okay if you don't want to come out. You stay in there as long as you like. *(He hangs his hat, turns off the t.v., puts down the flowers, lights a cigarette. Goes to the kitchen, checks the food in the oven.)* Your casserole smells nice. I think you got a good scald on it. *(Beat)* I wish I had a funny story about blind dates or casseroles, but I don't. *(Beat)* Maybe one will come to me later. *(Beat; to himself.)* Maybe not. *(He finds a radio on the kitchen counter, turns it on, flips the dial, finds a Hank Williams song.)* Hank Williams. From Oklahoma. I don't have a funny story about Hank Williams, either. Or Oklahoma. Well, Oklahoma's kinda funny anyway, right? I grew up lookin' at Oklahoma. From the south bank of the Red River. That's where I grew up. See, when I was a boy, the border between Texas and Oklahoma was actually the middle of the river. If you were fishing on the north bank, you were catching Okie fish. But I caught Texas fish. They probably tasted the same. Some time since then, we gave our half of the river away. Now the whole damn thing belongs to Oklahoma. South bank: that's the border. I'm not sure why we did that, but it makes me mad. Kind of like giving away your ... your front porch. *(DOTTIE emerges from her bedroom, wearing her jeans and sweatshirt.)* Good evening.

(She moves past him, into the kitchen, checks the food in the oven.)

DOTTIE. You said it was scalded.
JOE. No, I said, "You got a good scald on it." Just an expression.
DOTTIE. Oh.
JOE. How are you?
DOTTIE. Fine.
JOE. Do you want to know how I am?
DOTTIE. How are you?
JOE. I'm fine, thank you. *(JOE gets the flowers, gives them to DOTTIE.)* You look very nice.
DOTTIE. Thank you.

JOE. You're welcome.
DOTTIE. I changed.
JOE. Oh?
DOTTIE. I didn't know just you and me were gonna have dinner.
JOE. Somebody should've told you.
DOTTIE. They did. Just now.
JOE. What did you change from?
DOTTIE. A dress.
JOE. I'd love to see it.
DOTTIE. Are you hungry?
JOE. Famished. *(Beat)* Yes, hungry.
DOTTIE. Are you ready to eat?
JOE. Whenever you are.
DOTTIE. Your eyes hurt.
JOE. I beg your pardon.
DOTTIE. Huh?
JOE. May I have a beer?
DOTTIE. Oh, sure.
JOE. I'll get it.

(He gets a beer from the refrigerator.)

DOTTIE. Well ... I'll serve dinner.
JOE. That would be lovely.
DOTTIE. What did you say?
JOE. I said, "That would be lovely." *(She begins to set the table for two.)* Can I help you?
DOTTIE. No, that's okay.
JOE. How old are you?
DOTTIE. Twenty.
JOE. And Chris ... ?
DOTTIE. Twenty-two. *(Beat)* You're wonderin' about Daddy.
JOE. Hm?
DOTTIE. Daddy was sixteen when Chris was born. Momma was fifteen.
JOE. So young.
DOTTIE. It was an accident.

JOE. Really.
DOTTIE. They didn't want to get married.
JOE. Why did they?
DOTTIE. I don't know. That's just what they always said. "We didn't want to get married."
JOE. Do you trust me?
DOTTIE. Not quite.
JOE. Good.
DOTTIE. Have you ever been married?
JOE. Maybe.
DOTTIE. What does that mean?
JOE. It means no.
DOTTIE. How come?
JOE. Because women are deceitful, and lying, and manipulative, and vicious, and vituperative, and black-hearted, and evil, and old.
DOTTIE. *(Beat)* Yeah ...
JOE. What are you drinking?
DOTTIE. Nothing.
JOE. Can I get you something?
DOTTIE. No, thank you.
JOE. A tall glass of cold beer, perhaps?
DOTTIE. No, thank you.

(She finishes setting the table. She takes the casserole out of the oven, places it in the center of the table.)

JOE. Lovely.
DOTTIE. I'm a virgin.
JOE. I know.
DOTTIE. Okay.

(He helps her into her seat, lights a candle, places it on the table, turns off the lights, takes his seat.)

JOE. A. Tuna. Casserole.
DOTTIE. Yes.
JOE. May I serve?

DOTTIE. Please.

(He slices some casserole and puts it on her plate, then does the same for himself.)

JOE. It looks delicious.
DOTTIE. Thank you.
JOE. Thank you. *(He waits for her to take the first bite. She gestures, "After you." He takes a polite bite, eyes her, takes a larger bite, growls hungrily, and digs in. She begins eating.)* I'd really like to see that dress.
DOTTIE. It wasn't right.
JOE. May I see it anyway?
DOTTIE. How are you gonna kill Momma?
JOE. Ohhh ... that's not ... appropriate dinner conversation.
DOTTIE. Not unless you poison her.

(He freezes, food in his mouth. She laughs.)

JOE. I'm not sure I'm going to kill your mother.
DOTTIE. How come?
JOE. Because I rarely do that sort of thing. I have operatives.
DOTTIE. What's an operative?
JOE. An agent. An assistant.
DOTTIE. Oh.
JOE. Yes. Someone else will take care of it. *(Beat)* Unless, of course, I do it myself.
DOTTIE. So you might ... ?
JOE. Yes. I don't know.
DOTTIE. How will you do it? Or the operatives?
JOE. Well ... well, it'll be taken care of.
DOTTIE. When?
JOE. I don't know.
DOTTIE. Will you be the detective who investigates?
JOE. Probably not, but sometimes.
DOTTIE. Is that a problem?
JOE. That's a convenience.

DOTTIE. That's a convenience.

JOE. Yes.

DOTTIE. So are homes.

JOE. Yes.

DOTTIE. I love my brother. I remember when Momma and Daddy were havin' a divorce, and they, Momma had just told us (she was drunk), "I don't love your Daddy no more. I never loved him," and I screamed somethin' that didn't make any sense, and I ran out of the house, and into the yard, under the streetlight, and I was crying, Chris came out (he hadn't said anything), and he just ... laid on top of me. He stretched his body out, like this, and laid on me, until I stopped cryin' –

JOE. Dottie –

DOTTIE. – and we haven't talked about it, ever.

JOE. Bring the dress.

DOTTIE. Now.

JOE. Yes. *(They rise. She exits. A moment later, she enters, carrying the dress on a hanger.)* Why wouldn't you wear that for me?

DOTTIE. It's not me.

JOE. Not when you're not in it.

DOTTIE. I once had a boyfriend –

JOE. Put it on.

DOTTIE. *(Beat)* All right.

(She heads for the bedroom.)

JOE. Where are you going?

DOTTIE. I'm going to put the dress on –

JOE. I said put it on.

DOTTIE. I was –

JOE. Here.

DOTTIE. I –

JOE. Put it on, please. *(She hesitates.)* Put it on, Dottie. *(She lays down the dress, takes off her sweatshirt, hesitates again.)* I want to see you put it on. *(She takes off her tennis shoes. He stares at her. She peels off her jeans.)* Stop. *(She stops.)* Take off your socks. *(She does. He turns his back to her.)* Take off your brassiere. *(She hesitates.)*

Take off your brassiere. *(She does ... lets the brassiere fall to the floor ... covers her breasts ... then drops her arms to her sides.)* Take off your underwear.

(She does.)

DOTTIE. *(Very softly.)* Babies.

(His back is still turned to her.)

JOE. Put on the dress. *(She pulls the dress over her head.)* Come here. Right behind me. *(She does. He unfastens his belt and opens his pants.)* Reach around and put your hand in my pants.

(She does.)

DOTTIE. I don't remember ...
JOE. Do you feel that?
DOTTIE. Yes ...
JOE. What does that feel like?
DOTTIE. I don't remember ...
JOE. How old are you?
DOTTIE. Twelve.
JOE. So am I. *(Stillness, then:)* Switch places with me. *(She moves in front of him. Their eyes do not meet.)* Your boyfriend?
DOTTIE. Marshall.
JOE. Marshall.
DOTTIE. He was fat ...
JOE. Uh-huh ...
DOTTIE. He loved me. With a pure love. *(JOE slowly begins to lift her skirt.)* Our secret.
JOE. Nobody.
DOTTIE. Home.

(Blackout.)
(End of ACT I.)

ACT II

Scene One

(Lights slowly rise: late at night.)
(Thunder. Lightning. Footsteps. T-BONE.)
(CHRIS unlocks the door, but a metal chain keeps him from opening it. He moans, mutters.)
(He kicks the door open, snapping the chain off the wall. He staggers inside. His shirt and pants are soaked with blood. One eye is blackened, and blood streams from his nose and mouth.)
(Suddenly, KILLER JOE, naked and holding a gun, grabs CHRIS's hair from behind and forces him to the floor.)

JOE.
ALL RIGHT, GET DOWN THERE
NOW! GET DOWN!

CHRIS.
I'm sorry! I'm sorry!

(JOE relaxes, foot planted in CHRIS's back.)

JOE. Chris ...
CHRIS. Oh, fuck ...

(SHARLA, wearing a tee-shirt and a pair of men's underwear, runs in from the hallway. ANSEL is behind her.)

SHARLA. What the hell – ? *(She turns on the light and CHRIS's condition is visible to all of them.)* Good God, what happened – ?
ANSEL. You look rough, boy –
JOE. Excuse me.

(JOE exits to DOTTIE's bedroom. SHARLA and ANSEL keep their distance from CHRIS, examining him from across the room.)

41

CHRIS. Dad – ?
ANSEL. Them old boys caught up to you.
CHRIS. – my hand –
SHARLA. What happened?
CHRIS. I think they broke my hand –
ANSEL. What'd they do to your face – ?
CHRIS. I got –
SHARLA. – Jesus –
CHRIS. – I got –
ANSEL. You wanna go to the hospital – ?
SHARLA. I think he better –
CHRIS. I got beat up –
ANSEL. I can see that –
CHRIS. Oh, God –

(DOTTIE enters, wearing a robe. She rushes to CHRIS. JOE emerges again, now wearing a pair of slacks.)

DOTTIE. What happened to you?
CHRIS. Some guys –
DOTTIE. *(To SHARLA.)* Will you get a wet rag?
CHRIS. – I got beat up –

(SHARLA gets a dishrag, soaks it and wrings it out.)

ANSEL. They do all they were goin' to, or – ?
CHRIS. Huh – ?
ANSEL. Did they – ?
JOE. If they'd wanted to kill him, he'd be dead.

(SHARLA gives the dishrag to DOTTIE, who gently wipes blood from CHRIS's face.)

CHRIS. Oh, God –
DOTTIE. Your nose is broken –
JOE. Is that all?
CHRIS. What the fuck, man – ?

ANSEL. What'd they say to you?

CHRIS. What the fuck you think they said?

ANSEL. They want their money.

CHRIS. No shit.

SHARLA. You want a beer?

JOE. Where'd they find you?

CHRIS. Wild Bill's. They jumped me in the parking lot.

ANSEL. *(Stepping over CHRIS to turn on t.v.)* D'ja see Bill there?

CHRIS. I don't ... I don't know, why?

ANSEL. He owes me ten bucks.

CHRIS. Christ –

SHARLA. I'm goin' back to bed –

DOTTIE. *(To CHRIS.)* You sure you don't wanna go to the hospital?

CHRIS. Yeah, I –

SHARLA. C'mon, Ansel –

DOTTIE. That cut on your head looks pretty deep –

JOE. He's fine. He just got a whipping.

CHRIS. *(To JOE.)* Listen, buddy, I'm –

JOE. No, I'm saying, it could happen to anybody –

ANSEL. We'll turn in then, I guess –

SHARLA. Ansel, come on –

CHRIS. Just go –

ANSEL. – all right –

SHARLA. – good night –

CHRIS. Dottie –

(SHARLA exits.)

DOTTIE. You feel any better – ?

CHRIS. I didn't mean –

JOE. Come on, Dottie, you should get back in bed.

CHRIS. Wait just a minute here –

SHARLA. *(O.S.)* ANSEL!

ANSEL. Okay, goddamn it, I'm comin'.

(ANSEL exits.)

    JOE. *(To DOTTIE.)* Come on, Dottie.

    CHRIS. Dottie, I want to tell you: I never meant –

    JOE. Dottie. *(She stands and exits without turning back. To CHRIS.)* Good night.

(JOE turns off the light and goes to bed. CHRIS is left in the middle of the floor, bleeding by the light of the television.)

    CHRIS. *(Calling off.)* Joe? *(Beat)* We need to talk.

    JOE. *(O.S.)* Tomorrow.

    CHRIS. Now.

    JOE. *(O.S.)* It can wait.

    CHRIS. Right now.

(JOE reemerges from the bedroom, turns on the light, turns off the t.v.)

    JOE. Shoot.

    CHRIS. I wanna know what kinda progress you're makin' on your job.

    JOE. It's being taken care of.

    CHRIS. Yeah, it sure as hell is. You been here a week now, fuckin' my sister, and my mother's a helluva lot healthier than me at the moment.

    JOE. Cut to the chase, Junior.

    CHRIS. I'm havin' second thoughts.

    JOE. You want me off the job?

    CHRIS. I don't know –

    JOE. Say the word.

    CHRIS. Huh?

    JOE. Say the word. Your call.

    CHRIS. When are you plannin' on doin' it?

    JOE. Tomorrow.

    CHRIS. Really?

    JOE. Yes.

    CHRIS. How?

    JOE. I won't tell you.

CHRIS. Where?

JOE. I won't tell you.

CHRIS. Am I the customer here?

JOE. Tomorrow. That's all you need to know.

CHRIS. So you'll be leaving tomorrow.

JOE. No, of course not.

CHRIS. Why not?

JOE. The retainer isn't for the job. It's for the money. I'm not leaving until I get my money.

CHRIS. I don't like that.

JOE. I don't care.

CHRIS. I don't want you near my sister.

JOE. I don't care.

CHRIS. And if I tell you the deal's off –

JOE. I'll leave right now and you'll never see me again. Your call.

CHRIS. "Say the word."

JOE. Who are you into for this money?

CHRIS. I won't tell you.

JOE. Digger Soames?

CHRIS. How'd you know that?

JOE. Digger Soames. What did he say he'd do to you if you don't pay him?

CHRIS. You know that too?

JOE. He'll do it. I used to work with an old boy on the force ... can't remember his name. He and Digger came to cross purposes. Digger warned him; he didn't believe Digger would really do it. He went to sleep one night ... woke up six feet under. We found him a couple of months later ... like this:

(JOE mimics the position of a man found buried alive: hands hooked into claws, eyes and mouth wide open.)

CHRIS. Why didn't you arrest him?

JOE. I like Digger.

CHRIS. Aren't you supposed to arrest people who commit murder?

JOE. Where would you suggest I start, Junior?

CHRIS. Do it.

JOE. What are your plans for tomorrow?

CHRIS. Why?

JOE. Don't be around here tomorrow.

CHRIS. I'll be wherever the hell I feel like –

JOE. For the safety of the job ... make yourself scarce. Do you understand?

CHRIS. You'll never get my mother to set foot in this trailer –

JOE. Do you understand?

CHRIS. Yeah, but you'll never get my mother to set foot in this trailer.

JOE. You let me worry about that.

CHRIS. Okay.

JOE. Okay. Get some sleep.

(JOE starts for the bedroom.)

CHRIS. Joe? *(JOE stops, turns.)* You better not hurt my sister. *(JOE laughs.)* What's so funny?

JOE. Oh, I don't know. That just ... struck me.

(DOTTIE enters.)

DOTTIE. How many?

JOE. How many what, sweetie?

CHRIS. (sweetie?)

DOTTIE. I'm sorry, it's been a long time ...

CHRIS. She's asleep.

DOTTIE. You'd fuck a snake if you could hold it's head.

(JOE turns to CHRIS and smiles.)

JOE. That's fun.

(JOE puts his arm around DOTTIE and pulls her down the hallway.)

CHRIS. Dottie ...

(Blackout)
(Sound of the evangelist from the next scene plays over the blackout.)

Scene Two

(Lights rise: daylight streams through the windows.)
(KILLER JOE sits at the kitchen table, listening to an evangelist on the radio. His gun lays on the table.)
(T-BONE barks crazily. Pounding on the door. JOE lifts his gun, cocks it.)

CHRIS. *(O.S.)* Joe?! Joe?! *(CHRIS rushes in, sweating, out of breath, panicked. His head and hand are bruised, bandaged. JOE holsters his gun.)* Ah, thank God! I was afraid ... I wouldn't get here, and ... it'd be too late ... ah, thank God ... Listen. We gotta stop this thing. We can't ... *(CHRIS turns off the radio.)* I been in a lotta trouble, all my life, but I never tried nothin' like this before. I'm sorry. I didn't mean to waste your time. I hate that bitch. I've always hated her. I just ... I can't be the one, y'know? But more than that, the main thing, really, is, is, is Dottie. I mean, my sister ... she never did nothin' to nobody, y'know? And for me to ... I can't be ... responsible. And you can't have her. I can't let you have her. You gotta give her up, cause I can't look her in the eyes otherwise. Do you understand, Joe? I don't want my sister to see you again. I don't think you're a good influence. I mean, come on, Joe, you kill people, for Chrissake. Y'know? No offense. I mean, it's not like me and Dad or Mom have been especially good influences. But Dottie managed to turn out all right anyway. And it just seems like the best thing I can do for her now is to keep her away from people who won't do her any good. So I think it'd be best if you and me just shook hands and forgot any of us ever met. Is that okay? Can't we walk away from it before it goes too far? None of us are any better off, but we're really no worse off, either. I'm no better off. I owe Digger Soames six thousand dollars. I'll never have that kinda money, not ever. And, you know, even if I had it, wouldn't that suck, handin' it over to these guys? I'd wanna keep that money, try to make somethin' with it. I tried startin' a farm once. That seemed like the kind of life I want. Workin' for myself, outside a lot, make my own hours, live in the country, smoke dope, watch t.v. That's all I really want. So I started a rabbit farm. I built the whole thing, by myself. I was livin' with a couple guys out near Mesquite, but they didn't help me; I built it, with my own two hands. Lumber, chicken wire, water bottles, pellets. Rabbits. I loved those little bastards. They smell like shit, and they fuck all the time, but they're awful easy-goin' animals. I left for a couple weeks, cause of this girl down in Corpus, and when I got back, a rat, or a skunk, or somethin' had got in the pen, and it was rabid. Awful hot out, too. They just tore each other apart. Their eyes were rollin', and foamin' at the mouth, and ... and screamin'. Did you know rabbits can scream? They sound just like little girls. It was disturbing. I started sellin' dope for a living. I knew more about it. *(JOE checks a beeper affixed to his belt, then goes to the door, looks outside.)* So I can't pay this guy, and I don't even really want to. That means you gotta get out, Joe. You gotta get outta here, and leave my sister alone forever. Otherwise, you and me're gonna have some trouble. Do you understand? Do you understand?

(A long silence. CHRIS slowly turns and looks at a large, overstuffed garbage bag sitting by the other garbage in the kitchen. CHRIS walks to the bag, starts to open it ...)

JOE. Don't open it. Do you want to help me get her in the car?

(Blackout.)
(Sound of the Road Runner cartoon from the next scene plays over the blackout.)

Scene Three

(The lights slowly rise.)
(Daylight streams through the windows.)
(CHRIS staggers back and forth from the bedroom to the living room, doing a poor job of selecting mourning clothes. DOTTIE watches a Road Runner cartoon, and the volume seems incredibly loud.)

(CHRIS reaches his limit and snaps off the television.)

CHRIS. Goddamn coyote!

DOTTIE. I was watchin' that, Chris ...

CHRIS. Listen, honey –

DOTTIE. I was watchin' the show.

CHRIS. I know –

DOTTIE. I wanted to see how it turned out.

CHRIS. He doesn't catch the bird, okay?! It just goes on and on and on!

DOTTIE. Yeah?

CHRIS. Dottie. I know you know what's goin' on. I don't have to tell you anything; you know.

DOTTIE. Uh-huh.

CHRIS. I want you to understand somethin', though: I didn't mean to hurt you. I never meant to do that.

DOTTIE. Yeah ...

CHRIS. Arrangements just kinda broke funny, and ... if I had known how all of this was gonna fall out, I might've done things a little different.

DOTTIE. No ...

CHRIS. Well, maybe not, but I might have. Anyway, this's just about over and he'll be gone soon.

DOTTIE. He will?

CHRIS. Soon as this money comes through, and we pay the son-of-a-bitch –

DOTTIE. That's where they are now?

CHRIS. Dad and Sharla. Yeah, they're talkin' to Kilpatrick.

DOTTIE. He won't pay them today, will he?

CHRIS. Nah, they're just goin' over the policy –

DOTTIE. Joe's not leavin' just yet, right?

CHRIS. No, but soon, and then you won't ever have to see him again.

DOTTIE. See him ...

CHRIS. We're gonna be better off after this, honey. I'm gonna get outta this trouble I'm in, set things right. Get a job. Get married. I'm gonna do things right, from now on. I've gotta pay for things I've done wrong. You don't pay for that kinda stuff, and it comes back to you. Always.

DOTTIE. Uh-huh ...

CHRIS. Dad'll be able to ... oh, I don't know, you know Dad.

DOTTIE. Yeah.

CHRIS. And Dottie, you're finally gonna get to go to that modelin' school. You remember how you always wanted to do that? Like those girls in the thing?

DOTTIE. Christie Brinkley ...

CHRIS. Maybe you don't like me so much anymore. Maybe you don't think I did right by you, but by God, I did the best I could. Nobody can accuse me of not havin' people's best interests at mind. People do the best they can. Anybody says he doesn't's lyin'. *(Beat)* I did the best I could. I didn't want to hurt anybody. Ever. *(He grabs her, buries his head in her lap. She holds him.)* Oh, God ... fire ...

DOTTIE. Will there be a trial?

CHRIS. Huh?

DOTTIE. Will there be – ?

CHRIS. I don't know. I don't know. I doubt it. Joe knows what he's doin' –

(T-BONE barks.)

DOTTIE. I never been to a trial.

CHRIS. D'ja see the shot in the paper? Her car?

DOTTIE. Uh-huh.

CHRIS. Yeah, he knows what he's doin'. They couldn't even do a real autopsy cause there wasn't much left to speak of – *(ANSEL and SHARLA enter, wearing mourning clothes. CHRIS pulls away from DOTTIE.)* How'd it go?

ANSEL. You little bastard ...

CHRIS. What?

ANSEL. You little son-of-a-bitch ...

CHRIS. What's the matter?

ANSEL. I'm not talkin' in front of Dottie –

SHARLA. Oh, hell, Ansel, she knows what's goin' on –

ANSEL. I'm not talkin' in front of her!

CHRIS. What are you talkin' about? What happened with Kilpatrick?

ANSEL. Sharla, take Dottie for a drive –

SHARLA. You take her –

CHRIS. Will you please tell me – ?

ANSEL. I'm not talkin' in front of –

DOTTIE. They're not gonna pay you the money, are they?

(Silence)

CHRIS. Dad?

SHARLA. Tell him, Ansel.

CHRIS. Tell me.

SHARLA. Tell that idiot –

CHRIS. Just tell me –

ANSEL. Who told you about Adele's policy?

CHRIS. Rex. Rex told me. He just mentioned it. In conversation.

ANSEL. Rex ...

CHRIS. Will you for the love of God tell me – ?

ANSEL. When did he tell you?

CHRIS. In conversation –

ANSEL. Not how! WHEN!

CHRIS. A couple weeks ago. Me and Mom had just had a big fight –

ANSEL. Oh, Christ –

SHARLA. I told you, Ansel.

CHRIS. What happened?

SHARLA. I told you from the start –

CHRIS. Shut up, Sharla –

SHARLA. Don't tell me to shut up, I'm not the one who blew this thing – !

CHRIS. What happened, Dad?

SHARLA. You come in here – !

CHRIS. Dad?

SHARLA. – tell people what do to, how we're all gonna see a hundred grand – !

CHRIS. *(Advancing on ANSEL.)* Goddamn it, you tell me, right now –

ANSEL. Dottie is not the beneficiary. Rex is the beneficiary.

CHRIS. I don't understand.

ANSEL. It's not real tough –

CHRIS. Explain it to me.

ANSEL. Dottie does not get the money. Rex gets the money.

CHRIS. Wait, I –

ANSEL. Dottie does not get the fifty thousand dollars. Rex gets the fifty thousand dollars.

CHRIS. That's not right.

ANSEL. That's the way it is.

CHRIS. That can't be.

ANSEL. Go talk to Kilpatrick yourself.

CHRIS. That can't be. I don't – what do you, what do you – what do you mean? Because I was told! Because – because I was told! Because Rex told me! He told me! Rex told me!

DOTTIE. Rex was Momma's boyfriend –

CHRIS. JUST – SHUT UP, DOTTIE! He told me –

SHARLA. He was lyin'.

CHRIS. Why would he do that?

SHARLA. Why do you think?

CHRIS. No, no, he couldn't've known! He couldn't've know I'd do this!

SHARLA. He's the one who put the idea in your head –

CHRIS. I don't fucking believe this –

ANSEL. Who told you about Killer Joe?

CHRIS. *(It hits him.)* Oh ... oh, God ...

SHARLA. *(To ANSEL.)* I told you. Did I tell you?

ANSEL. Yeah ...

CHRIS. Oh my God ... I'm fucked ... piece of fucking fuck suck cake ...

ANSEL. He really played you like an accordion fish, didn't he, boy?

CHRIS. No, God –

SHARLA. *(To CHRIS.)* You make me sick.

CHRIS. I don't believe you, God –

(ANSEL grabs CHRIS, shoves him, holds him.)

ANSEL. Well, you better believe it. Sooner you start believin' it, sooner you can figure a way to pay Killer Joe his money –

SHARLA. We gotta get goin' –

ANSEL. – not to mention Digger Soames –

SHARLA. We gotta get goin', y'all.

ANSEL. What for?!

SHARLA. Funeral's in half an hour.

CHRIS. You all go ahead. I gotta think of somethin'.

ANSEL. Oh, I wish you would. We always seem so much better off when you do.

DOTTIE. Where's Joe? Isn't he going to the funeral?

SHARLA. No, huh-uh.

DOTTIE. He's comin' back, isn't he?

CHRIS.	ANSEL.
Yeah ... yeah, he's comin' back, all right.	Oh, he's comin' back.

ANSEL. Let's hit it. We gotta get your mother in the ground.

CHRIS. I'll take Dottie.

ANSEL. Dottie?

DOTTIE. We'll be along.

ANSEL. All right. Mrs. Smith? *(SHARLA is spraying her thighs with some cheap perfume.)* When you're done fumigatin' the Gates of Hell. *(She exits. ANSEL follows, stops at the door. To CHRIS.)* Hey. Why don't you do us all a big favor and kill yourself?

(They're gone. T-BONE barks.)

DOTTIE. You feel bad.

CHRIS. Yeah, I do ... I think maybe I'm not supposed to be on Earth or somethin' ...

DOTTIE. You remember those shows you used to put on? With your knees?

CHRIS. Hm?

DOTTIE. We'd be lyin' in bed, late at night, and you'd get a flashlight, and put your knees up, and you'd put a pair of sunglasses on one knee, and some kind of hat on the other?

CHRIS. Yeah ...

DOTTIE. And you'd put on a little show. "The Greatest Show on Earth." That's what you called it.

CHRIS. Yeah ...

DOTTIE. "Into Time and Forever From Now On. No Ventures, or Time-Outs, or King's-X's, Everlasting, One More Than You Can Say, Into Infinity, and Outer Space. Amen."

CHRIS. Nothin's worse than regrets. Not cancer, not bein' eaten by a shark, nothin'.

DOTTIE. Joe is comin' back, isn't he? Cause I think maybe I'm –

CHRIS. I'm leaving.

DOTTIE. I think maybe I'm –

CHRIS. Will you come with me?

DOTTIE. (his eyes hurt)

CHRIS. I'm leaving. And I want you to come with me.

DOTTIE. Where?

CHRIS. Mexico. No. Further. Peru. In South America.

DOTTIE. How do we get there?

CHRIS. We'll drive. We can drive it. Dottie, we can do this. It may not be livin' it up, exactly, not for a while – do you like Texas? I never liked this goddamn state. You hear these people talk about it like it's such a great place and all, but it's really just a bunch of goddamn hicks and rednecks with too much space to walk around in.

DOTTIE. It's warm.

CHRIS. Let's go. Let's just ... go. Now.

DOTTIE. To the funeral.

CHRIS. No, Dottie, listen, if we're gonna pull this off, we gotta gas up –

DOTTIE. I have to see Joe.

CHRIS. No, no, Dottie, if we see Joe –

DOTTIE. I have to see him.

CHRIS. We have to go to Peru *now*.

DOTTIE. Then you go by yourself. I have to see Joe.

CHRIS. All right, I'll make you a deal. We'll go to the funeral, and you can see Joe.

DOTTIE. Good.

CHRIS. But you can't tell him we're plannin' on leavin'. You can't tell him good-bye. Not outright.

DOTTIE. Okie-doke.

CHRIS. And you can't tell Dad or Sharla either, cause they're mad at me right now and they might try to screw up our trip.

DOTTIE. Right.

CHRIS. We'll go to the funeral. You'll see Joe after.

DOTTIE. I understand.

CHRIS. Are you excited? Do you want to go?

DOTTIE. I'm always excited.

CHRIS. We can do this thing, Dottie. We can pull it off.

DOTTIE. Not if somebody makes me mad.

CHRIS. What?

(Blackout)
(Sound of thunder during the blackout.)

Scene Four

(The lights slowly rise.)
(The daylight is dark blue and fading. [By the end of the scene, it should be dark outside.] The lights inside the trailer are off.)
(No one is on stage.)
(Thunder. Lightning. T-BONE.)
(Footsteps. A moment later, the door opens and SHARLA and ANSEL enter, still wearing their funeral clothes. SHARLA carries a bucket of fried chicken.)

ANSEL. It's dark.

SHARLA. Dottie?! It's us!

ANSEL. I can't find the light. *(SHARLA turns on the lights, sets the chicken down in the kitchen. ANSEL empties his pockets of keys, wrappers, lint, a pint bottle, and a mountain of change onto the kitchen table. He struggles out of his coat and shirt, then turns on the t.v.)* Christ ...

SHARLA. Dottie?! We stopped by the K-Fry-C! You hungry?! *(Beat)* Dottie?! *(Beat)* Chris?!

ANSEL. Fetch me a beer.

(JOE emerges from Dottie's bedroom.)

JOE. He's not here.
ANSEL. Hi, Joe –
SHARLA. Is Dottie here?
JOE. She's asleep.
SHARLA. Where's Chris?
JOE. I don't know.
SHARLA. You want some chicken? Stopped by the K-Fry-C.
JOE. Yes, please.
SHARLA. Help yourself. It's on the stove.
ANSEL. Get it for him, would you, hon?
SHARLA. Sure. White or dark?
JOE. Leg.
SHARLA. You need a plate?
JOE. No, thank you.

(She wraps a chicken leg in a paper towel and hands it to him.)

ANSEL. Want a beer?
JOE. Yes, please.
ANSEL. Honey, would you – ?

(She gets beers for ANSEL and JOE, then gets a piece of chicken for herself. ANSEL grabs his pint from the kitchen table, offers JOE a swig.)

SHARLA. Funerals make people hungry for some reason.
JOE. Hm.
SHARLA. I'm starvin'.
JOE. *(Beat)* Hm.
SHARLA. *(Beat)* Dottie told you about the insurance.
ANSEL. Sharla –
JOE. Yes. She did.
ANSEL. *(To JOE.)* I don't know what to say.
SHARLA. You don't have to say anything. Not your fault.
ANSEL. Yeah, but –

SHARLA. *(To JOE.)* Chris. That Chris is so stupid. I coulda told you he'd fuck things up.

JOE. Why didn't you?

SHARLA. Why didn't I?

ANSEL. *(To JOE.)* Just an expression, really.

JOE. What is?

ANSEL. Well ... what she said. That she coulda told you he'd fuck it up.

JOE. I've never heard that expression.

ANSEL. Manner of speakin', is what I mean –

SHARLA. I've never liked that little bastard.

JOE. You haven't.

(During the following, JOE collects ANSEL's discarded clothing, carries it off, down the hall.)

SHARLA. You can't trust him. He's just no good.

ANSEL. They never really hit it off –

SHARLA. All he cares about is himself.

ANSEL. That's not fair, really –

SHARLA. Bullshit fair. It's true.

ANSEL. Well, that's all anybody really cares about, isn't it?

SHARLA. No wonder.

ANSEL. No wonder what?

SHARLA. No wonder Chris wound up like he did.

ANSEL. What did I do?

SHARLA. Just shut up –

ANSEL. Hey, now –

SHARLA. *(To JOE, as he reenters.)* I mean, how stupid do you have to be to let an idiot like Rex take advantage –

JOE. Rex.

SHARLA. Yeah, Rex ...

JOE. What about Rex?

SHARLA. I said ... I said, "How stupid do you have to be to let an idiot like Rex –"

JOE. Yes, I heard what you said. Tell me about Rex.

ANSEL. *(To JOE.)* Rex is Adele's boyfriend.

JOE. Was.

ANSEL. Was Adele's boyfriend –

JOE. *(To SHARLA.)* Tell me about Rex.

ANSEL. What do you want to know – ?

JOE. *(To ANSEL.)* Not you. *(To SHARLA.)* You.

SHARLA. What.

JOE. You. Tell me about Rex.

SHARLA. What do you mean?

JOE. You know the man, right? I mean, you've met him.

SHARLA. Yeah, of course –

JOE. Tell me about him.

SHARLA. I don't know what you –

JOE. Is he tall? Is he fat? Is he Chinese? Where does he work? How old is he? Do his ears hang low? Is he unlike other men? Tell me about Rex.

SHARLA. Uh ... Rex is ... I don't get this, really –

JOE. Who told you about our arrangement?

SHARLA. What arrangement?

JOE. The contract made between myself and this family. Who told you about it?

SHARLA. Ansel.

JOE. Why?

ANSEL. Joe, she's my wife, you know –

JOE. I wasn't addressing you, sir.

ANSEL. Okay.

JOE. Why did he tell you?

SHARLA. Cause I'm his wife, like he said, he tells me –

JOE. Were you supposed to get a cut of this money?

SHARLA. Sure –

JOE. Why?

SHARLA. Why?

JOE. Why?

SHARLA. Cause – cause I'm his wife, like he said –

JOE. Did you advise Ansel against the idea?

SHARLA. No –

JOE. Why? You could've told him Chris would fuck it up.

SHARLA. It's none of my business –

JOE. But it is, isn't it? It is your business.

SHARLA. Look, what is this all – ?

JOE. If you were going to share in the money, it is your business. Isn't it?

SHARLA. Yeah, I don't know –

JOE. Yet you didn't advise against it.

SHARLA. No. No, I didn't.

JOE. Why not?

SHARLA. I'm trying to tell you –

JOE. Why didn't you advise against it?

SHARLA. Cause I wanted some of that money, all right? I mean, if, if Chris could pull something like that off –

JOE. Were you going to split Ansel's third? Or were the four of you going to split it up evenly?

SHARLA. We didn't discuss that –

JOE. Oh, now, I'm sure you did. You're a practical woman.

SHARLA. I don't know, I assumed I would take ... a fourth –

JOE. Not one-half of one-third –

SHARLA. No, one fourth, four ways –

JOE. – instead of one sixth –

ANSEL. – one-sixth –

SHARLA. No, four ways, to even –

JOE. So then the four of you would –

SHARLA. Right –

JOE. – would split the remainder of the money, after I had been paid –

SHARLA. Right –

JOE. – paid my fee of twenty-five thousand dollars –

SHARLA. Uh-huh, after you were covered –

JOE. What?

SHARLA. I say, after you were covered –

JOE. Which means, equal shares, you wanted that money, what would those four equal shares come out to, that's –

SHARLA. I haven't done the math –

JOE. Well, then, do it with me, now. *(During the following, JOE takes a seat at the kitchen table and uses ANSEL's pile of change to visualize his calculation. SHARLA reluctantly joins him.)* The insurance policy gets covered, the agent, Kilpatrick, cuts you a check, or cuts Ansel a check –

SHARLA. – Dottie, that would be –

JOE. – right, best of all possible worlds, Dottie –

SHARLA. I don't even know why we're goin' over all this, since we're not –

JOE. Please, just watch my feet here, all right – ?

SHARLA. All right –

JOE. So Ansel gets the –

SHARLA. Dottie –

JOE. – Dottie –

SHARLA. If the check is for a hundred, we pay you twenty-five –

JOE. How much?

SHARLA. – twenty-five –

JOE. But how much, the policy was for – ?

SHARLA. However much. *(To ANSEL.)* How much?

ANSEL. Fifty-thousand.

SHARLA. That much, so fifty minus your twenty-five –

JOE. Right, minus my twenty-five, but you said a hundred, didn't you?

SHARLA. A hundred what?

JOE. You said a hundred, the check is for a hundred –

SHARLA. However much, minus your twenty-five, leaves twenty-five four ways –

JOE. But you said a hundred.

SHARLA. Yeah. However much.

ANSEL. She was mistaken. It's fifty.

JOE. Is it?

ANSEL. Yeah. *(A long silence. JOE rises from the table, turns off the television.)* Idn't it?

JOE. No.

ANSEL. Wait a minute ...

JOE. In case of accidental death ... the figures double.

SHARLA. Oh, right, Kilpatrick told us that this morning. Didn't he, Ansel?

ANSEL. Huh-uh.

SHARLA. Yeah, I think he did.

JOE. Ansel? Did he?

ANSEL. No.

SHARLA. I think he did –

ANSEL. So ... it's not ... fifty.

JOE. No. *(To SHARLA.)* It's a hundred.

SHARLA. Like I say. However much.

JOE. However much.

SHARLA. Look, what are you gettin' at?

JOE. What do you mean?

SHARLA. I made a mistake, all right – ?

JOE. Yes, you did –

SHARLA. – so it's fifty, or a hundred, or however much –

ANSEL. Hey, you all don't do this now –

JOE. You said you never cared for Chris –

SHARLA. – and I haven't. I don't –

JOE. – and you said Rex is an idiot –

SHARLA. uh-huh, right –

JOE. – and you said, "the check is for a hundred" –

SHARLA. – "or however much" –

JOE. – and I was just wondering –

SHARLA. – what are you gettin' at – ? *(JOE reaches in his pocket and takes out the rainbow-colored packet that Sharla had at the beginning of Act One, Scene Three.)* – oh, fuck –

(He takes the sheaf of photographs from the packet and shows one to SHARLA.)

JOE. Whose dick is that?

SHARLA. Where'd you get those?

JOE. That's not Ansel's dick, I bet. *(He hands one of the photographs to ANSEL.)* Is that your dick?

ANSEL. No.

SHARLA. Oh, hell, yes it is, darlin', you were drunk –

JOE. *(Showing ANSEL another photo.)* How about that one?

ANSEL. No.

JOE. That one? Make sure now. Might've been drunk. *(ANSEL shakes his head. Examining a photo.)* So whose dick is that? Is that your little step-son's cock in your mouth?

SHARLA. Just stop it –

JOE. Or does that particular dick belong to your boyfriend?

SHARLA. Please –

JOE. To your boyfriend: Rex: "That idiot."

SHARLA. Please, now, just –

JOE. The man who's getting all that money.

SHARLA. I didn't –

JOE. All "hundred grand."

SHARLA. I said stop it –

JOE. That's a nice photo, really. You should frame that. *(To ANSEL.)* What do you think? Look nice on the bedroom dresser?

SHARLA. I didn't know, I swear –

JOE. *(To ANSEL.)* Were you aware of this?

ANSEL. I'm never aware –

JOE. Of course not. *(To SHARLA.)* Whose is it?

SHARLA. You son-of-a-bitch –

(JOE grabs her by the throat with one hand.)

JOE. There's no need for name-calling. I haven't called you any names. You be polite to me. I'm a guest. Now tell me whose little dickie that is, and don't lie to me or by God it'll be the last lie you ever tell.

SHARLA. Rex. It's Rex.

JOE. Correct.

SHARLA. Ansel, please –

JOE. Oh, I don't think Ansel is too inclined to give you any assistance at this point in time. Are you, Ansel?

ANSEL. No, I'm not.

JOE. In fact, you're content to just sit there, aren't you?

ANSEL. Yes, sir.

JOE. That's what I thought.

SHARLA. Let me go, you motherfucker –

(JOE tightens his grip on her throat.)

JOE. What did I say about insulting me?

SHARLA. *(Choking)* Let me go – I can't breathe –
JOE. What was that? I'm sorry, I can't quite hear you.
SHARLA. Let ... me ...

(DOTTIE emerges from the bedroom.)

DOTTIE. Joe?
JOE. Go back to bed, honey.
DOTTIE. Did you take out the trash?
JOE. No, but I will.
DOTTIE. Well, your eyes are just black as night.
JOE. All right, just go back to sleep.
DOTTIE. I can't sleep with Momma in there.

(She goes back into the bedroom. JOE relaxes his grip on SHARLA.)

SHARLA. We'll give you the money. I swear, I'll talk to Rex and we'll give you as much of the money as you want.
JOE. I'm afraid that's impossible.
SHARLA. No, it's not –

(ANSEL moves to the television.)

JOE. Rex picked up the settlement this afternoon.
SHARLA. What?
JOE. *(As ANSEL reaches t.v.)* Don't touch that television. *(JOE takes a cashier's check from his pocket.)* He gave it to me before he left. *(Hands check to ANSEL.)* "A hundred grand."
ANSEL. God amighty ...
SHARLA. Where did he go?
JOE. It's worthless, of course. Made out to Rex.
ANSEL. Oh my God ...
SHARLA. Where did he say he was goin'?
JOE. He was unavailable for comment.

(JOE peels off his watch and pockets it as he approaches SHARLA.)

SHARLA. I don't understand, why didn't you get him to – ? I can ... I can get him to sign it over –

(He punches her squarely in the face. She falls to her knees.)

JOE. Looks like you need a new boyfriend. *(She crawls away from him, toward ANSEL, toward the living room. He follows, puts the toe of his boot in her ass, pushes her down.)* I'll be your boyfriend. Just for a little while.

(JOE walks back to the kitchen, grabs another chicken leg.)

ANSEL. *(Terrified whispers to SHARLA.)* Stay down ... just stay down there ...

(JOE strides back to SHARLA. ANSEL shreds the check; a plead with JOE. JOE stands above SHARLA, holds the chicken leg in front of his crotch.)

JOE. Suck this.
SHARLA. Go fuck yourself –

(JOE reaches down, one-handed, grabs her hair, slams her head onto the floor, screams in her face:)

JOE. You insult me again, and I'll cut your face off and wear it over my own! Do you understand?!
SHARLA. *(Crying)* Ansel – !

(ANSEL rockets off the couch, about to attack. JOE drops SHARLA, spins to face ANSEL, who quickly retreats to the kitchen sink.)

ANSEL. Hey, you made your bed –
JOE. That's right. Now lie in it.
SHARLA. Ansel, please –
JOE. *(Grabbing her hair again.)* Are you going to insult me again?! Do you want me to wear your face?! *(Holding her head with*

one hand, the chicken leg in front of his crotch with the other.) Now suck it. *(Shaking, crying, she hesitantly takes the end of the chicken leg in her mouth.)* Ohhhh, yes ... *(To ANSEL.)* Hey. What do you think?

ANSEL. I don't.

(JOE bobs her head back and forth on the chicken leg.)

JOE. Now, you listen to me, and I want you to listen very carefully, both of you. I performed a service for this family, and I deserve my payment in full. As a result of the misunderstanding regarding the insurance, I'm not going to receive any cash for my services. And that's unfair. I don't care to hear excuses, or the placement of blame. I hold you all equally responsible. Reach around and grab my ass. *(She does.)* I was fortunate, however, in thinking ahead. I secured a retainer for my services. Since I fulfilled my obligation, and since my cash is not forthcoming, that retainer is now mine. It belongs to me. And I'm taking it with me when I leave. *(He bucks his hips, jams the bone further into her mouth. She is sobbing.)* You're very good at this. Please moan. *(She begins an awkward humming.)* Chris doesn't agree with the concept of the retainer. He's coming back here tonight and he's going to attempt to take it with him. I can't allow him to do that. This family can't allow him to do that. *(He's now ramming the bone into her mouth up to its hilt. He finally groans and pushes the chicken leg all the way in. She gags. He gasps, lets her go. She falls to the floor, coughs out the leg.)* Do you understand?! If this family allows Chris to leave this trailer, I'll slaughter all of you! Like pigs! Do you believe I'd do that?! *(He drops to the floor, straddling her. She screams.)* I'm asking for your help. Will you give it to me? *(She nods.)* Ansel?

ANSEL. Yes, sir.

JOE. Good. *(He traces a finger around SHARLA's breasts.)* You know, you're a very beautiful woman. *(To ANSEL.)* Don't you think so?

ANSEL. I haven't given it much thought –

(JOE places the point of his finger over her windpipe.)

JOE. No. Wrong answer.

ANSEL. *(Weeping)* Yes. She is a very beautiful woman.

JOE. *(To SHARLA.)* That's sweet. Don't you think so? *(She nods. He grabs her under the arms and hoists her to her feet.)* Now, get your ass in that kitchen and set the table for a proper meal. Then we'll all sit down and eat. Just the four of us. Just the family. *(She moves away slowly. He playfully whacks her on the ass; she runs to the kitchen sink and vomits. ANSEL sits at the kitchen table. JOE lights a cigarette.)* How are you, guy?

ANSEL. Where'd you get them photographs?

JOE. Oh, that's hardly important.

ANSEL. I guess ...

JOE. All she did was suck his cock and try to steal your money. It could've been worse.

ANSEL. How?

JOE. *(Beat)* Well, no. I suppose that's about as bad as it gets. *(Then, privately:)* Spend time with your wife.

(JOE exits down the hallway.)

ANSEL. Sharla ...

SHARLA. Yes?

ANSEL. Are you okay?

SHARLA. Yes, Ansel, I'm fine.

ANSEL. Are you sure?

SHARLA. Yes, I'm sure.

ANSEL. Okay. *(He weeps. T-BONE barks.)* He's home.

(CHRIS enters the trailer.)

CHRIS. Hey there.

ANSEL. Hello, son.

CHRIS. Dottie here?

ANSEL. She's in the bedroom.

CHRIS. *(Eyeing the chicken bucket.)* Thank God, I'm starvin'. You hear from Joe?

ANSEL. He's in the bedroom.

(CHRIS picks up the chicken leg from the floor, carries it into the kitchen.)

CHRIS. *(To SHARLA.)* You eat already?

(DOTTIE comes out of the bedroom.)

DOTTIE. Hi, Chris.

(JOE emerges from the bedroom.)

JOE. JUNIOR! YOU'RE HOME!
CHRIS. Hi, Joe.
JOE. Hey, I heard about the money, and I gotta tell you, I'm all broke up things didn't work out –
CHRIS. – yeah, me too –
JOE. – but that's the way the world turns, right?
CHRIS. Huh – ?
JOE. That's the way the cookie crumbles?
CHRIS. Yeah, okay –
JOE. Caveat emptor, you know what I mean? *(SHARLA rakes change, keys, everything from the kitchen table onto the floor.)* A place for everything. *(Extends his arm to DOTTIE.)* Shall we dine? *(She takes his arm and he ushers her to the table. SHARLA sets the table with paper plates and the bucket of chicken.)* It smells heavenly. Ansel? Chris? "K-Fry-C?"
ANSEL. I'm not hungry, really ...
JOE. You should join us, though. All of us. *(The family gathers at the table and takes their seats. SHARLA continues setting the table with paper towels and plastic silverware.)* Come on, Sharla, take your seat. *(She does.)* Let me see if I can scare us up some music. *(He turns on the radio, finds music. Stands back, observes the family at the table.)* This is lovely. *(Takes his seat.)* Who would like to say grace? *(No response.)* Dottie? Will you do the honors?

(The family clasps their hands, lowers their heads. They do not close their eyes.)

DOTTIE. Dear Jesus, Thank you for the food. Thank you that we're all here, together, and safe. We're sorry Momma's dead. We hope you'll give her a place to stay in Heaven. Please forgive us for anything we did wrong. We would all like a place to stay in Heaven, too. In the Lord's name which is Jesus Christ, we say, "Amen."

JOE. Amen. *(To DOTTIE.)* That was beautiful.

DOTTIE. Thank you.

JOE. *(To all.)* Let's eat. Sharla, we need some drinks, please. *(They eat. SHARLA gets plastic cups, a plastic pitcher of iced tea, a case of beer from the fridge, a carton of non-dairy creamer. The others pass chicken, mashed potatoes, coleslaw. JOE directs the action, asking for iced tea, passing the food around, commenting on the meal, directing SHARLA to finally sit and eat. The others respond as they are addressed [although SHARLA is silent]. Finally, JOE taps his iced tea cup with a plastic "spork," stands, and extends his cup.)* I have an announcement to make: You've all probably noticed by now that Dottie and I have been spending an awful lot of time together. The fact is: we've fallen in love. So it's my privilege to tell you that I've asked her to be my bride. And she has accepted. Isn't that true, dear?

DOTTIE. Yes.

(Silence)

ANSEL. Well, I, for one, am very happy for –

CHRIS. Shut up.

JOE. A toast: to my future wife.

(JOE drinks. All but CHRIS follow suit.)

CHRIS. When's all this supposed to take place?

JOE. *(Taking his seat.)* We're leaving after this delicious meal.

CHRIS. *(To DOTTIE.)* Is that right?

DOTTIE. Yes.

CHRIS. You can't have my sister, Joe.

JOE. What do you mean?

CHRIS. I mean I can't let that happen. You're not going to marry my sister. You can't have her.

ANSEL. Now, Chris, I don't think it's up to you –

CHRIS. Shut up.

ANSEL. Don't tell me to shut up –

CHRIS. Say another word, old man, and I'll rip your head off your shoulders.

JOE. Chris, I can certainly appreciate your love for your sister, but you have to cut the old apron strings sometimes –

CHRIS. I'm not gonna discuss it. She's my sister. I'm takin' her with me. We're leavin' here.

JOE. Maybe we should let Dottie decide –

CHRIS. Dottie doesn't have a say in the matter.

JOE. I believe she does –

CHRIS. You believe wrong. Dottie, go get your stuff.

JOE. *(To DOTTIE.)* Stay seated.

CHRIS. Dottie?

JOE. Dottie. *(She stands.)* Take your seat, Dottie.

CHRIS. Go get your stuff.

JOE. Take your seat.

CHRIS. Dottie?

(She walks toward the bedroom.)

JOE. Dottie.

CHRIS. Go on, Dottie –

JOE. Stop –

CHRIS. Dottie, go get your stuff, now –

JOE. Dottie.

CHRIS. That a girl –

(She reaches the hallway.)

JOE. *DOTTIE!!! (She stops in the doorway.)* She's my retainer.

CHRIS. The deal's off.

JOE. No, it's not.

CHRIS. It didn't work out. You're gonna have to eat this one.

JOE. You know ... you know I'll kill you.

CHRIS. Go fuck yourself. *(Silence. JOE drops his napkin on his plate, slowly stands up from the table. CHRIS raises his hand from beneath the table. He is holding a .45. ANSEL and SHARLA jump from the table, back into the kitchen. He cocks the gun, steadies it with his left hand, keeps it aimed at JOE's head.)* Take your seat, Joe. *(JOE slowly sits down as CHRIS rises and backs around the table.)* Get your stuff, Dot –

(SHARLA grabs a knife from the kitchen counter, screams, buries it in CHRIS's upper chest, near his shoulder. The knife handle snaps off in her hand. CHRIS reels, shocked. The gun fires, striking the floor.)

(JOE flips the table over, charges CHRIS, buries his shoulder in CHRIS's stomach, and drives him into the wall. The gun flips out of CHRIS's hand into the living room. DOTTIE picks it up.)

DOTTIE. Stop it!
JOE. *YOU'RE DEAD, MOTHERFUCKER! YOU'RE DEAD!*

(JOE grabs the lamp cord, wraps it around CHRIS's neck, and heaves. Choked, dazed, CHRIS flies into a kind of seizure, doing anything he can to get free.)

DOTTIE. Stop it, Joe! Stop it!
JOE. *DEAD! DEAD! DEAD!*
DOTTIE. STOP IT!
JOE. ANSEL, GRAB HIS LEGS!

(ANSEL falls on CHRIS's kicking legs, holds them tight under his arm. CHRIS looks in horror at his father as the three men writhe toward the living room.)

ANSEL.	DOTTIE.
I GOT HIM, JOE – !	STOP IT, DADDY – !

(SHARLA grabs a potato peeler from the sink and charges at CHRIS, who tries to twist his body out of the path of the blade. She sticks the potato peeler blade in his side, one, two, three times.)

(CHRIS flails, kicks off ANSEL. JOE flings him around the room by the cord, smashing him into cabinets, counter, table, television, refrigerator.)

JOE. *DIE, MOTHERFUCKER, DIE!*
DOTTIE. *(Shrieking, hysterical.)* STOP IT, STOP IT, GOD!
ANSEL. HOLD HIM STILL, GODDAMN IT!

(CHRIS backs up suddenly, smashing JOE against the wall. JOE loosens his grip momentarily and CHRIS elbows him sharply in the ribs. JOE gasps, lets go of the cord, falls to the floor. CHRIS approaches DOTTIE, his hand out.)

CHRIS. Dottie, the gun –

(ANSEL grabs CHRIS from behind, picks him up, squeezes him, throws him into the kitchen. SHARLA smashes a beer bottle over CHRIS's head. ANSEL shoves him into the refrigerator, holding him down.)

DOTTIE. GOD, STOP IT, PLEASE, STOP IT!

(CHRIS flails inside the refrigerator. Shelves, beers tumble out of the fridge.)

ANSEL. JOE, KILL HIM! I GOT HIM! *(CHRIS tries to struggle out of the refrigerator, but JOE is suddenly there, beating hell out of CHRIS.)* SHARLA, GRAB HIM – !
JOE. *GODDAMN YOU, DIE!*

(SHARLA jumps on CHRIS's feet, pins them to the floor. ANSEL holds CHRIS down while JOE continues beating on him.)

ANSEL. DO IT, JOE, KILL HIM!
SHARLA. KILL HIM! KILL HIM!
DOTTIE. I'M GETTING ANGRY!
JOE. *DIE, DIE, DIE!*

(DOTTIE fires the gun, striking the radio. JOE, ANSEL, and SHARLA immediately roll out of the way and look at DOTTIE. CHRIS pulls himself out of the refrigerator and looks at her also. She points the gun at him.)

CHRIS. Dottie?

(She fires, strikes him squarely in the chest, rockets him back into the refrigerator. SHARLA screams.)

ANSEL. Jesus – *(DOTTIE pivots, shoots ANSEL in the stomach. He falls to his knees, clutching the hole in his stomach. Blood spills from his mouth. SHARLA screams again.)* Oh, my Christ, honey ...
SHARLA. *(Hysterical)* DON'T KILL ME, DOTTIE! *(SHARLA scrambles behind ANSEL, wraps her arms around him.)* PLEASE DON'T LET HER KILL ME!

(JOE starts toward DOTTIE. She pivots, points the gun at his head.)

JOE. Now, Dottie ... just take it easy. *(He advances. She aims carefully.)* Hold on, now. Be safe. *(He advances. She cocks the gun.)* Oh, God ...

(She tenses, squeezing the trigger slightly.)

DOTTIE. I'm gonna have a baby.

(JOE looks at her, uncertain.)

JOE. A baby? *(Beat)* A baby? *(He smiles broadly, proudly ...)* A baby!

(ANSEL holding his stomach, SHARLA crying behind him, JOE smiling, DOTTIE with her finger tensed on the trigger, CHRIS dead in the refrigerator.)
(Blackout)

SKIN DEEP
Jon Lonoff

Comedy / 2m, 2f / Interior Unit Set

In *Skin Deep*, a large, lovable, lonely-heart, named Maureen Mulligan, gives romance one last shot on a blind-date with sweet awkward Joseph Spinelli; she's learned to pepper her speech with jokes to hide insecurities about her weight and appearance, while he's almost dangerously forthright, saying everything that comes to his mind. They both know they're perfect for each other, and in time they come to admit it.

They were set up on the date by Maureen's sister Sheila and her husband Squire, who are having problems of their own: Sheila undergoes a non-stop series of cosmetic surgeries to hang onto the attractive and much-desired Squire, who may or may not have long ago held designs on Maureen, who introduced him to Sheila. With Maureen particularly vulnerable to both hurting and being hurt, the time is ripe for all these unspoken issues to bubble to the surface.

"Warm-hearted comedy … the laughter was literally show-stopping. A winning play, with enough good-humored laughs and sentiment to keep you smiling from beginning to end."
– *TalkinBroadway.com*

"It's a little Paddy Chayefsky, a lot Neil Simon and a quick-witted, intelligent voyage into the not-so-tranquil seas of middle-aged love and dating. The dialogue is crackling and hilarious; the plot simple but well-turned; the characters endearing and quirky; and lurking beneath the merriment is so much heartache that you'll stand up and cheer when the unlikely couple makes it to the inevitable final clinch."
– *NYTheatreWorld.Com*

SAMUELFRENCH.COM

COCKEYED
William Missouri Downs

Comedy / 3m, 1f / Unit Set

Phil, an average nice guy, is madly in love with the beautiful Sophia. The only problem is that she's unaware of his existence. He tries to introduce himself but she looks right through him. When Phil discovers Sophia has a glass eye, he thinks that might be the problem, but soon realizes that she really can't see him. Perhaps he is caught in a philosophical hyperspace or dualistic reality or perhaps beautiful women are just unaware of nice guys. Armed only with a B.A. in philosophy, Phil sets out to prove his existence and win Sophia's heart. This fast moving farce is the winner of the HotCity Theatre's GreenHouse New Play Festival. The St. Louis Post-Dispatch called Cockeyed a clever romantic comedy, Talkin' Broadway called it "hilarious," while Playback Magazine said that it was "fresh and invigorating."

Winner!
of the HotCity Theatre GreenHouse New Play Festival

"Rocking with laughter...hilarious...polished and engaging work draws heavily on the age-old conventions of farce: improbable situations, exaggerated characters, amazing coincidences, absurd misunderstandings, people hiding in closets and barely missing each other as they run in and out of doors...full of comic momentum as Cockeyed hurtles toward its conclusion."
–Talkin' Broadway

SAMUELFRENCH.COM

ANON
Kate Robin

Drama / 2m, 12f / Area

Anon. follows two couples as they cope with sexual addiction. Trip and Allison are young and healthy, but he's more interested in his abnormally large porn collection than in her. While they begin to work through both of their own sexual and relationship hang-ups, Trip's parents are stuck in the roles they've been carving out for years in their dysfunctional marriage. In between scenes with these four characters, 10 different women, members of a support group for those involved with individuals with sex addiction issues, tell their stories in monologues that are alternately funny and harrowing..

In addition to Anon., Robin's play What They Have was also commissioned by South Coast Repertory. Her plays have also been developed at Manhattan Theater Club, Playwrights Horizons, New York Theatre Workshop, The Eugene O'Neill Theater Center's National Playwrights Conference, JAW/West at Portland Center Stage and Ensemble Studio Theatre. Television and film credits include "Six Feet Under" (writer/supervising producer) and "Coming Soon." Robin received the 2003 Princess Grace Statuette for playwriting and is an alumna of New Dramatists.

BLUE YONDER
Kate Aspengren

Dramatic Comedy / Monolgues and scenes
12f (can be performed with as few as 4 with doubling) / Unit Set

A familiar adage states, "Men may work from sun to sun, but women's work is never done." In Blue Yonder, the audience meets twelve mesmerizing and eccentric women including a flight instructor, a firefighter, a stuntwoman, a woman who donates body parts, an employment counselor, a professional softball player, a surgical nurse professional baseball player, and a daredevil who plays with dynamite among others. Through the monologues, each woman examines her life's work and explores the career that she has found. Or that has found her.

THE OFFICE PLAYS
Two full length plays by Adam Bock

THE RECEPTIONIST
Comedy / 2m, 2f / Interior

At the start of a typical day in the Northeast Office, Beverly deals effortlessly with ringing phones and her colleague's romantic troubles. But the appearance of a charming rep from the Central Office disrupts the friendly routine. And as the true nature of the company's business becomes apparent, The Receptionist raises disquieting, provocative questions about the consequences of complicity with evil.

"...Mr. Bock's poisoned Post-it note of a play."
— *New York Times*

"Bock's intense initial focus on the routine goes to the heart of *The Receptionist's* pointed, painfully timely allegory... elliptical, provocative play..."
— *Time Out New York*

THE THUGS
Comedy / 2m, 6f / Interior

The Obie Award winning dark comedy about work, thunder and the mysterious things that are happening on the 9th floor of a big law firm. When a group of temps try to discover the secrets that lurk in the hidden crevices of their workplace, they realize they would rather believe in gossip and rumors than face dangerous realities.

"Bock starts you off giggling, but leaves you with a chill."
— *Time Out New York*

"... a delightfully paranoid little nightmare that is both more chillingly realistic and pointedly absurd than anything John Grisham ever dreamed up."
— *New York Times*

SAMUELFRENCH.COM

CPSIA information can be obtained at www.ICGtesting.com
Printed in the USA
LVOW10s1926061214

417553LV00034B/1873/P